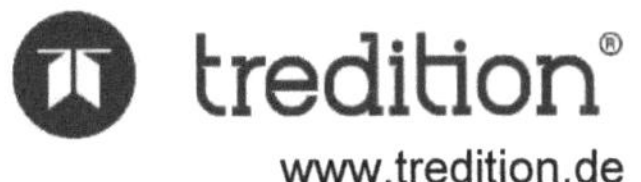

Dr. Anna Rostomyan is an Assistant Professor of English, Corporate Communications Consultant, Researcher, Author, Coach and Reviewer at Sage Publishing. Her PhD work, which she defended back in 2013 in tight collaboration with the University of Fribourg, Switzerland, Department of Philosophy and Interfaculty Institute for Central and Eastern Europe, being awarded an ASCN PhD research grant, and Yerevan State University, English Philology Department and Chair of English for Cross-cultural 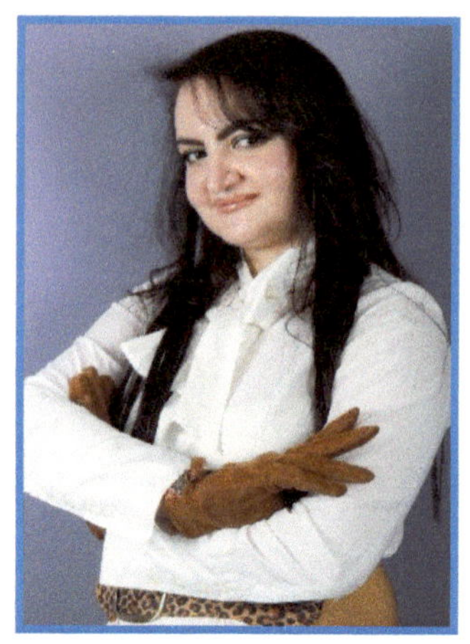 communication, was devoted to the linguo-cognitive, pragmatic, neurolinguistic, and psycholinguistic analysis of the verbal and non-verbal expression of emotions in English fiction and films.

While interested in a whole range of disciplines as Pragmatics, Psycholinguistics, Sociolinguistics, Neurolinguistics, Cognitive Linguistics, Communication Studies, and Discourse Analysis, her current research and studies are mainly focused on Emotional Intelligence, Neuroeconomics, Neuroleadership, Personal Branding, Emotional Marketing, Business Communication Management, etc.

Apart from academia, she also consults companies with successful communication and recruitment strategies, among which "Porsche Center Yerevan", "ArmenOil", and "Armeconombank" OJSC.

This book is particularly meant for the Business world professionals, leaders and for the Communication Science specialists to have a better understanding of communication management issues, self-awareness, self-management, social competence and especially emotional intelligence. The present book is the result of about 10 years' research work, elucidating the main findings of the author in the field of Communication Science.

Author contact: annarostom@yahoo.com

Dr. Anna Rostomyan

Business Communi-cation Management

The Key to Emotional Intelligence

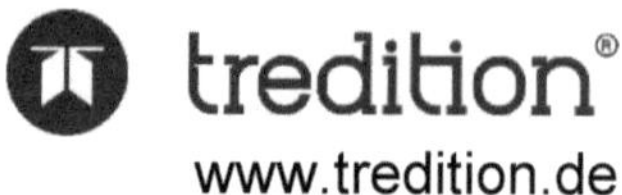

Verlag und Druck:
tredition GmbH, Halenreie 40-44, 22359 Hamburg

ISBN
Paperback: 978-3-347-20842-1
Hardcover: 978-3-347-19711-4
e-Book: 978-3-347-20843-8

CONTENT

COMMUNICATION IS THE KEY

*****Business** environment progressively grows multifaceted where human capital becomes the only sustainable source of competitive advantage for any organization, especially in these times of digitalization in terms of New Leadership and New Work.*

In today's globalized and capitalized world, it has become an urgent issue to seek for ways of healthy and efficient emotional communication management and communicative conflict minimization for the benefit of healthy interactions and effective labour output.

*The **present book**, composed of two correlated sections, gives an overall presentation on communication issues, as well as a minute depiction of the vitality of emotions at workplace and in everyday life. It suggests different ways both for professionals and beginners to reach peaceful interpersonal relations, which will consequently greatly contribute to successful business development, as well as to strong, effective and peaceful interrelations.*

*This is a step-by-step **guide**, which gives you deep knowledge on communication management issues and emotional intelligence.*

Preface

Business environment increasingly grows multifaceted and multicultural, where human capital becomes the only sustainable source of competitive advantage for any organization. Communication mainly consists in coding and decoding information on diverse issues with the people whom we encounter on various occasions. It is the mutual exchange of understanding with the receiver of the information.

When talking about Business Management, we first of all have to speak about effective communication, which is the essence of productive management as we deal with human beings. The basic functions of management, such as Decision Making, Planning, Organizing, Staffing, Directing and Controlling, cannot be performed efficiently and thoroughly without effective communication.

Business Communication actually involves instant and constant flow of information. Communication indeed plays a very important role in the process of directing and controlling the people in each and every organization. Hence, there should be effective communication between superiors and subordinated employees in any organization by means of flat hierarchical operation systems, as well as between an organization and the society at large, since it is also very essential for the development of success and the growth of an organization (Ternès & Rostomyan, 2011b).

Although it might sound trivial or even irrelevant to bring up such basic matters as language, meaning, interpretation and communication, these are the most fundamental components of *arguments* — even more fundamental than *propositions*, *inferences*, and *conclusions*. We cannot make sense of an argument without being able to make sense of the language, meaning, and purpose of what is being communicated in the first place. Hence, the present book will give a glimpse into diverse relevant components of communication so that to have a better understanding of it, as in case you have an idea of the processes going beyond communication, you will become better communicators.

In fact, language is a subtle and complex instrument used to communicate an incredible number of different things, but for our purposes here we can reduce the universe of communication to four basic categories: *information, direction, emotion*, and *ceremony*. The first two are often treated together because they express cognitive meaning while the latter two commonly express emotional meaning.   Language, indeed, is the basic means of communication between human beings. And just as it is the basic form, it is also the most developed one. We cannot communicate in any real sense without language, other than through gestures, facial expressions, bodily movements, and some other non-linguistic means; we also do communicate through some other non-verbal forms like the visual arts, e.g.: painting and sculpture, through dance, architecture, engineering, fashion, design, and the like, yet the culmination of true, articulate, communication is undoubtedly being realized via language. Actually, language has an irreplaceable role in our life, since it is very crucial in building successful and peaceful relations in our society, and business is not an exception.

As far as the relation of *logic* and *emotion* is concerned, Cicero tended to place a greater emphasis upon the emotive language rather than the logical. He points out to the fact that very often the decisions of those who decide greatly depend on the level of emotionality of the speaker. He does not claim that it is a disadvantage and should thus be avoided. Just on the contrary, he even advises that:

"Men take a decision oftener through feeling than through fact or law. They are moved by evidences of character in the speaker and in his client. The only way to rebut feeling is by feeling." (Cicero, 1895: 178)

Thus, the communication of information may be the most frequently viewed as thought-of use of language, where emotions play a vital and sometimes even a dominant role and place of which should not be underestimated. Though undeniably the basic means of conveying information is through statements or propositions, namely the building blocks of arguments, some of the "information" here might not be true because not all arguments and felicity conditions are always valid; however, for the purposes of studying logic, information being conveyed in a statement may be either false or true depending on the extralinguistic features, and, thus, the decoding process of emotional information can be really very challenging. Yet, in case **credibility**, **trust**, **loyalty**, unique **style** and **individual identity** are intermingled, every business is sure to flourish.

The present book studies the role of emotion in speech, their essence, as well as the expression and management of outward displays of emotions across cultures and situations, studying diverse emotion expression management techniques for the benefit of communicative conflict reduction and interpersonal peaceful relations, especially in the business environment.

This work outlines the importance of Emotional Intelligence (EQ) as an addition to your IQ (rational quotient) in the business cluster and other spheres of human activity. In fact, your emotional intelligence lies in your ability in efficiently handling your very own emotions, understanding your own and the emotions of the others, communicating your emotions effectually, empathizing with others, overcoming challenges, stress and communicative conflict; thus, helping you in building peaceful and harmonious, successful and effective relationships.

Having conducted a thorough interdisciplinary linguo-cognitive, psycholinguistic, neurolinguistic, sociolinguistic, phonetic, and pragmalinguistic analyses, we mainly take into consideration the supreme and subtle role of emotions in our lives, which are not here viewed as mere sensations, but rather special phenomena containing rational elements, which interplaying with one another altogether build our higher cognitive processes.

The next section gives you an idea about communication and emotion management techniques, which help you raise your EQ.

Section One

Communication and Emotions

1.1. The Ways of Business Communication

The rules, regulations and policies of a company have to be communicated to the people within and outside the organization. Business Communication is regulated by certain rules and norms. In early times, business communication was limited to paper-work, telephone calls, etc. Yet nowadays, with the advent of high technology, all the employers and employees have cell phones, organize video conferences, especially in terms of globalization and digitalization, make constant exchange business news via emails, etc.

Nowadays, Business Communication is generally realized via the below mentioned two types of communication, i.e.:

1. *Oral Communication* – an oral communication can be formal or informal. Generally business communication is a formal means of communication, like: meetings, interviews, calls, group discussion, debates, speeches, presentations, etc.
2. *Written Communication* – written means of business communication includes: agenda, reports, minutes, manuals, emails, letters, etc.

Today, within each and every company communication is not only made in real life, but also on the web. As a matter of fact, there is a common assumption that face-to-face communication is more persuasive, much clearer which makes a relationship much stronger as during face-to-face communication is much more calculable than during on-line communication, since while vis-à-vis conversing with your social partners one stands a better chance of having the desired emotive impact on the listeners via using non-verbal means of communication as well, that is body language which fits to the words used by the speaker supplying the counterpart with extra information about the latters emotional states and eventually having an emotive impact on the listener, whereas in the process of network communication there is a potential lack of showing one's emotions on the vocal and non-verbal level, namely voice modulations, facial expressions, bodily gestures, etc. Of course, one can make use of diverse emoticons for email, instant messages, social blogs and mobile phones to express positive or negative emotions, but there is always the problem on the part of the receiver to decode whether a particular smiley was meant to be sincere and to show the exact emotion that the sender of the message was fostering at the moment of displaying it, or whether it was used just as a means of emotion management for the sake of preserving harmonious social interpersonal relations (Rostomyan, Ternès, 2011a,b). Indeed, it is a very difficult task for each and every one of us to grasp the real *speaker meaning* – whether while face-to-face or on-line communication, as we are always being influenced by our previous emotional experience, which is embodied in our mental world as emotional background knowledge (Rostomyan, 2012).

The linguistic expression of emotions has to do with pragmalinguistic approach to language phenomena. It is also noteworthy that emotions reflect the speaker's state as well as his/her intention, emotions, feelings, or the communicative goal. As we know, for communication people have different emotion management techniques which help them to build successful social relationships. Emotions may be expressed in gross bodily movements and facial expressions; however, one's emotional state is basically expressed in speech (Rostomyan, 2009).

It should be stated that communication is composed of three interrelated phases:
- Verbal Communication;
- Non-verbal communication;
- Visual Communication.

In terms of Business Communication, as compared with Social Communication, Visual Communication comes to the fore as here a number of important issues are being communicated via visual gadgets such as various ads, blanks, costumes, etc., especially in Marketing Communication, which may vary across cultures and situations. As a matter of fact, by means of Visual Communication the producers may slightly suggest which kind of emotions should be revealed in the minds of the decoders of the provided information.

It is a well-known strategy when wanting to have an emotional influence on the audience the producers and content makers adhere to different famous story-tellings with a happy ending, which, when re-minded, evoke in the minds of the spectators positive emotions.

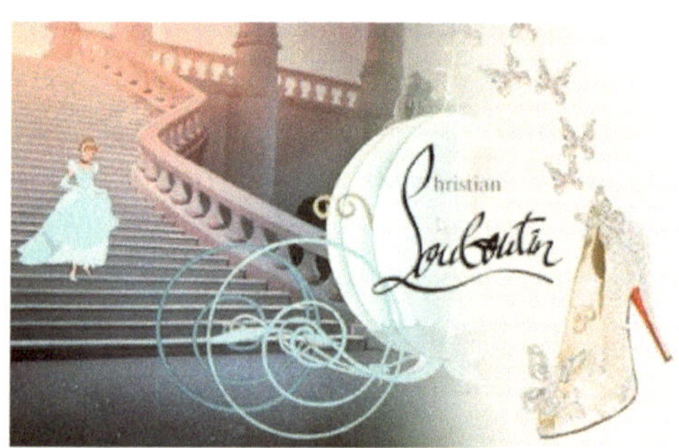

For instance, the very well-known French footwear designer **Christian Louboutin**, whose footwear has incorporated shiny, red-lacquered soles that have truly become his signature managed to at-tract the attention of and have a positive emotive impact on the ladies worldwide by his new col-lection, which embodies laced shoes that resemble to those of Cinder-ella. To attract much wider space of consumers and to raise the demand in the markets of his product, he referred to the story of Cinderella, her image and the following slogan: *"Cinderella is proof that a new pair of shoes may change your life"*.

Picture source: http://styleyourselfprincess.blogspot.com/2012/09/christian-louboutin-cinderella-shoes.html

As a matter of fact, bringing examples of fiction and films en-hances the emotional effect on the audience and ensures better results, which bring opulence to the company. But one has to be careful not to create illusions and to present your brand in a novel and positive view for the customers not to get disappointed after purchasing the product.

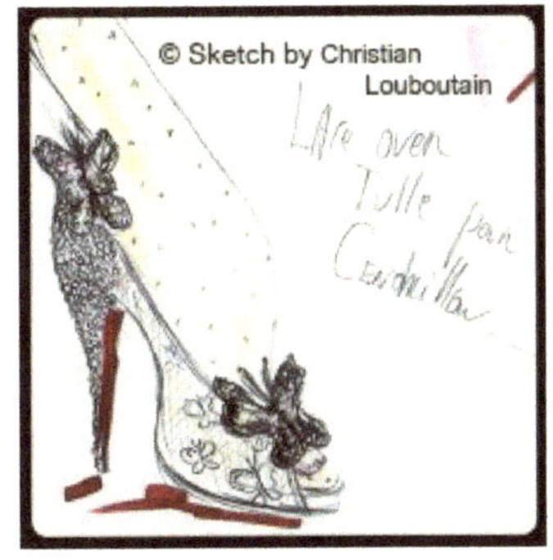

Hence, Louboutin, still to protect himself of misinterpretation, he also used the following design sketch of the shoes to defend himself from criticism of those, whose lives would not improve as a cause of the purchase. The red colour embodies pain and blood. This suggests that the inner beauty of the *"princess"* wearing the shoes has to match the beauty of the shoes to ensure *wealth, well-being, fortune* and *luck*. Also subtly suggesting that beauty sometimes needs sacrifice and that luxury may sometimes also be gained painfully.

Picture source: https://www.pinterest.com/pin/170996117072455350/

Truly many fashion industry moguls try to depict the story of Cinderella in their marketing ads to ensure better sales.

In fact, designers nowadays very often apply the prototype of fairy tales in their marketing strategies as people believe in miracles and, thus, the producers may reach their desired positive effect on the consumers. Such an instance can also be viewed on the ads of the mogul fashion company *"Hermès"*, the chief designers of which have also adhered to the "brand" notion of Cinderella as can be shown in this present shoe advertisement. Moreover, it should be noted that as a slogan for this line of advertisement they have chosen the following French slogan: *"La Vie comme un Conte/ Life as a Fairy Tale"*.

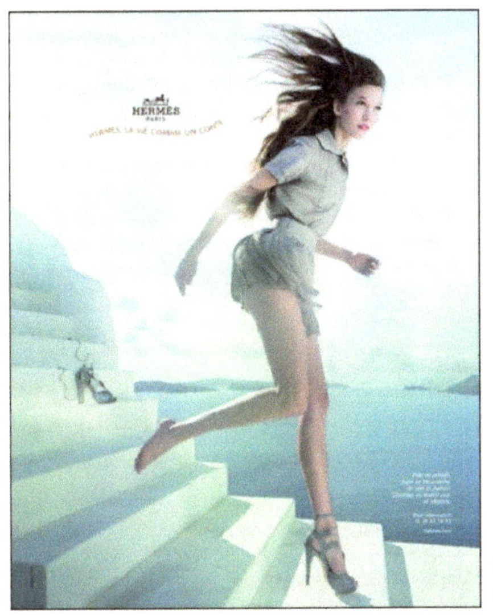

Picture source: https://www.pinterest.com/pin/402438916671890281/

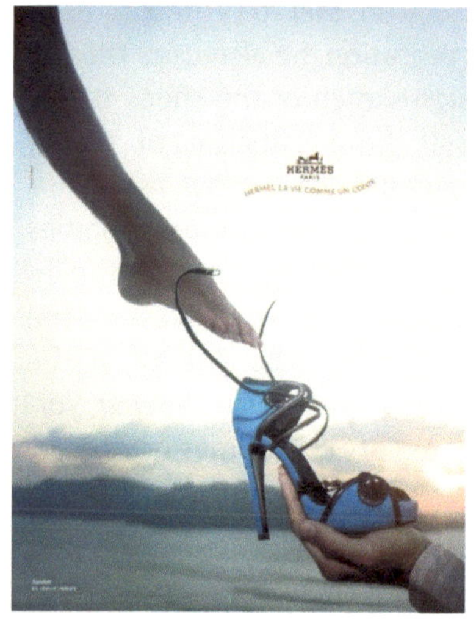

The following ads is also another example of the Hermes vogue line *"La vie comme un Conte/Life as a Fairy Tale"*, which well-illustrates a picture from the well-known Cinderella fairy tale, when the Prince tries to find the lady, who had lost her fairy shoe after the ball on the staircase. By means of testing all the ladies in town he tries to find the right one. So, the designers of Hermes, when advertising the present shoe, subtly on the emotional subconscious level suggest that by means of buying this shoe you will also find your prince charming.

Picture source: https://www.pinterest.co.uk/pin/312226186650606675/

In this respect, the context of situation in which a communicative act takes place gains a very outstanding role. It was Malinowski who coined the term "context of situation" in 1923. He claimed that: "Exactly as in the reality of spoken or written languages, a word without *linguistic context* is a mere figment and stands for nothing by itself, so in the reality of a spoken living tongue, the utterance has no meaning except in the *context of situation*". (Malinowski, 1923: 307).

Indeed, language is always being applied in a multifaceted environment, which includes a great variety of items in itself and bears a very complex background, which has to be taken into consideration in the process of information interpretation and cognitive analysis.

Actually, when we code and decode any piece of information, we are simultaneously performing a number of activities connected with 3 main aspects which are presented in the **Figure 1** drawn below:

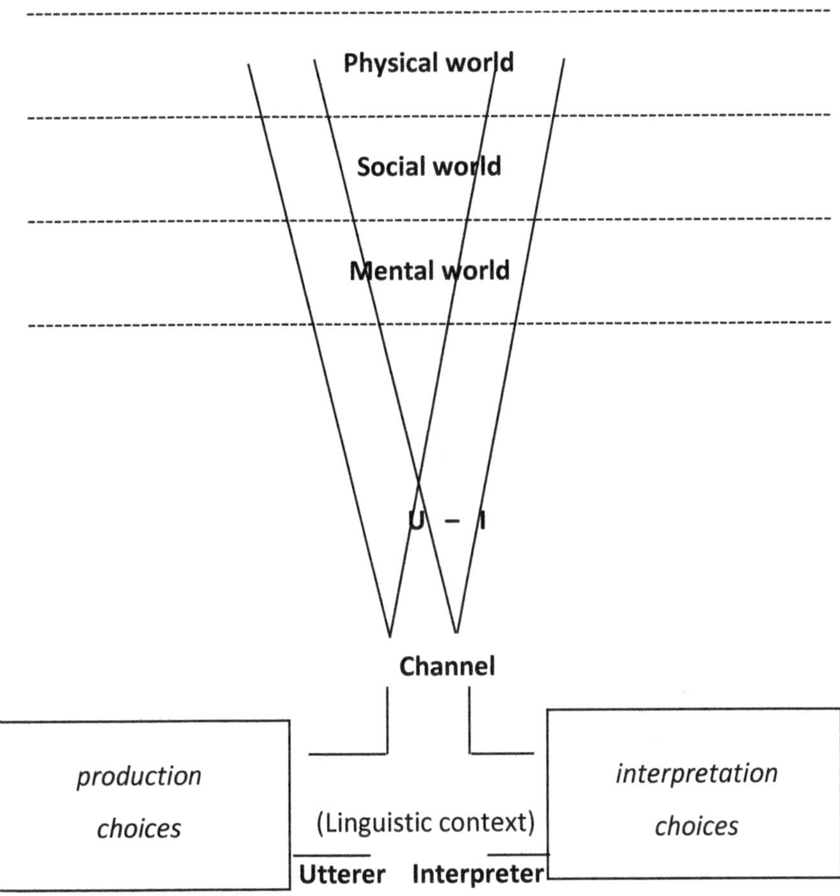

Figure 1: Contextual correlates of adaptability (Verschueren, 1999: 76)

This figure well-illustrates that in the process of communication it is not only the language channel that bears the responsibility of producing and evaluating the intended messages, but there are also some other important processes that partake in this process. As we see, the communicative context involves several ingredients which are: the mental world, the social world and the physical world. First of all, the information is being processed in the brain of the speaker. Secondly, he/she by means of language expresses those very thoughts explicitly or implicitly. But it is very important to note that there are a lot of other factors that have an impact on the individual while processing this or that information in the brain, which are respectively presented in the above designed figure. In fact, humans do not exist apart from each other, in other words we are not devoid of any social connection, and thus our **social world** is always participating in the process of communication. Here, **culture** is of paramount importance since a lot of factors connected with the social world are governed by means of a number of culturally bound rules and conventions.

If we go back to the interpretation of the marketing ads, we will see that all the aforementioned fields get fully activated in the complex process of information digestion.

As we know, in order to interpret what is being conveyed in an act of communication, we have to look at various factors, such as: social distance and closeness, especially in terms of Business Communication, and, thus, adhere to this or that *"rule of politeness"* not to sound rude, inconsiderate or impolite. For instance, to show the social distance between two people an English speaker who considers himself/herself as lower in status, uses forms of address that include a title and a last name, but never the first name, unless they are associates or friends (e.g., Mrs. Brown, Dr. Johnson, Pr. Bush, but not John or Steven). This greatly depends on cultural habits which are passed from generation to generation. Thus, we may conclude that each nation has its own *"principles of politeness"*. The above-mentioned examples illustrate the rules in English-speaking communities, whereas in Japanese there are much more forms of addressing which exactly reflect the distance between the interlocutors. Armenian, which, unlike English, has the "luxury" of singular and plural personal pronouns (դու – Դուք), reflects acts of politeness with the help of grammatical meaning of plurality. As Verschueren states: "[...] many linguistic choices depend on relationships of *dependence* and *authority*, or *power* and *solidarity*, not only between utterer and interpreter but also between utterer and/or interpreter and any third party which either figures in the topic of the discourse or is otherwise involved." (Verschueren 1999: 91, Rostomyan, 2013b)

Moreover, for some languages, the concept of *"social relationships"* may be extended to the extent that it can be applied to indicate relationships not only between human beings, but also between people and animals, people and plants, and even people and things. Thus, those very animals, plants and things become an indispensable part of our daily activities. This phenomenon can truly explain the sailor's choice of "she" as the pronoun, which is used to refer to a ship, or the choice of a driver to refer to the car by means of the same pronoun in the English language, a language which normally tends to make all lifeless things grammatically neuter. In fact, it should be kept in mind that all those community-specific communicative roles are strongly culturally-dependent and may vary across cultures. Thus, when being in a new cultural environment one should be able to learn at least the most basic communicative norms so that not to get in a ridiculous or confusing situation.

It is of utmost importance to note that we firmly believe human feelings and emotions to have an impact on our ***mental world*** and are very often being manifested in speech when we do not manage to suppress a particular emotion or when we want to have an emotive impact on the interlocutors, as mentioned in our earlier discussions, we display this or that emotion in an exaggerated manner. We will come back to the mental world a bit later and will give a much more detailed discussion on it.

Last but not least, our ***physical world*** is of utmost importance as well, since the relativity of temporal and spatial reference is primarily a function of positioning of language users in the world. As known, a lot of choice-making is dependent in these phenomena. In a number of cases the interlocutors' position in the physical world is important in determining a lot of linguistic choices and their meanings. The time during which an act of communication takes place is also very important, e.g.: from a variety of ways to greet each other in morning we choose to say "Good morning!" in English, "Guten Tag!" in German, "Bonjour!" in French, "Доброе утро!" in Russian, «Բարի առավոտ» in Armenian instead of saying "Good evening!", "Guten Abend!", "Bonsoir", "Добрый вечер!", or «Բարի երեկո»: Another interesting phenomenon, which can be observed in the German language is that there is a special way of greeting each other when it is time to have an evening meal, which is the greeting expression "Mahlzeit!". There are a lot of other ways how people depart from each other depending on the duration of the time when they will see each other again as in German "Bis bald!" which is equal in English to saying "See you soon!", "Bis gleich!" when the speakers will see each other after just a very short period of time, "Bis dann!" which is equal to saying "See you then!" in case both of the interlocutors know exactly when that very "then" will be, as well as many other similar expression. For instance, in French there are also some expressions denoting the meaning of "See you soon" as the expression "À tout à l'heure" and "À plus" or "À plus tard". Obviously, this is a phenomenon which is typical of almost all languages, since the factors of time and space are constant factors, which do not vary across cultures.

Thus, we have revealed that all these factors are involved in the process of communication and the focal points here, of course, are the utterer (U) and the interpreter (I). Without them, as well as without the functioning of their minds, there is no language use. Actually, in face-to-face interaction the roles of utterer and interpreter are continually interchanging and they constantly switch between different real-world people. It is also noteworthy that at any moment of the communicative act it is not unlikely for an utterer to become the interpreter of his or her own statement; this can be done in case the utterer himself or herself wants to analyze how the information that he or she has already coded can be decoded on the part of the interlocutor. Thus, we see that their roles are not so strictly separated from each other; nonetheless, it is obvious that any coded information requires interpretation. Notably, we distinguish between utterer and interpreter since the contextual aspects of the **physical**, **social**, and **mental worlds** do not usually start to play an eminent role in language use unless they have in this way or another been activated by the language users' cognitive processes. It is also very important to note that the elements of all the aforementioned worlds may overlap (Verschueren 1999).

In the figure, it is also indicated that for communication a specific linguistic channel is required. For verbal communication (in contrast to the use of sign language), only one linguistic channel is biologically given: speech sounds, or vibrations of the atmosphere produced with air from the lungs and by means of speech organs shared by the users of all human languages, i.e. the vocal cords and the vocal tract with a pharynx, glottis, uvula, tongue, soft and hard palate, alveoli, teeth, lips, and nasal cavity (Verschueren 1999: 103). Besides, as we know, we communicate with each other by not only linguistic means, but also by extra-linguistic means: bodily postures, gestures, facial expressions, etc. Sometimes even just a gaze may be sufficient to decode the intended meaning. Finally, **Figure 1** also indicates that the utterer makes production choices, whereas the interpreter makes interpretation choices.

We may generalize that all these aspects form parts a kind of background information for the interlocutors, which is a very important factor in the process of interpretation. In fact, background knowledge is central to any theory of pragmatics, sociolinguistics, discourse and context. It is a multifaceted, heterogeneous category which comprises a lot of diverse elements. We will focus our attention on the background mutual emotions between the interlocutors the formation of which is certainly connected with their mental world, as we do believe that ***emotional memory*** has a great impact in the decoding process. But first of all, we need to have a closer view on such a challenging and interesting notion as ***background knowledge*** which is otherwise also called background assumptions, background knowledge, common ground, mutual knowledge, etc. (Paronyan, Rostomyan, 2011b, Rostomyan, 2012).

When we think of the ways we use language, as we have already mentioned, we think of face-to-face conversations, telephone conversations, reading and writing, and even talking to oneself. These are arenas of language use - theaters of action in which people do things via language. But what exactly *are* they doing with language? What are their goals and intentions? By what processes do they achieve these goals? In order for one person to understand the other, there must be a kind of "***common ground***" of knowledge between them. This "common ground" from their past conversations, their immediate surroundings, their shared cultural background, as well as their knowledge about their emotions, beliefs, dreams and desires, is of utmost importance for building mutual understanding. In case there is some kind of mutual understanding between the speakers, this will lead to a drastic reduction of social conflicts.

The philosopher Jürgen Habermas has talked a lot about this issue. In his essay "What is Universal Pragmatics?" he suggests that humans should come to an understanding: by coming to an "understanding" he means at the very least that when two or more social actors share some meanings about certain words or phrases; and at the very most, when these actors are confident that those meanings fit relevant social expectations or a mutually recognized normative background (Habremas 1979: 3). In other words, we can say that in case people have shared knowledge on certain facts, beliefs, desires, emotions, etc. or on some other phenomena that are culturally bound, it becomes easier for them to understand each other even without going deep into details.

This section gave us a glimpse on the ways and forms of business communication, giving a detailed depiction of the communication processes and illustration on verbal, non-verbal, and visual communicative context of speech formation and information interpretation, by means of thoroughly analyzing the mental processes involved in speech encoding and de-coding, which are very important in both in everyday life situations and in Business Communication.

In case managers do communicate about their special demands and needs appropriately and openly, as well as manage the expression of their emotions, which will be thoroughly discussed in the next section, they will eventually stand a better chance of reaching their desired emotional effect and the positive predisposition of their employees.

1.2. Vitality of Trust and Emotion Expressions in Business Communication

Trust is an essential social, business and communicative notion, which is mainly aimed at a specific connection between two or more social interactants. Numerous definitions can be found in sociology, communication studies (Kohring and Matthes, 2007), as well as some other related disciplines. Despite some contradictory viewpoints and subsequent definitions there is a certain consensus on then basic meaning of trust, i.e. it is necessary and present when the actors (trusters) cannot or do not want to control the actions of their interactants, expecting a certain action on the part of these alteri (trustees) (Quandt, 2012: 8).

As we may guess, these expectations are primarily based on a past experience, which can be based on both a former personal life experience or any other experience connected with the same or similar actors under the same and/or similar circumstances and situations. Here, the mutually shared *emotional background knowledge* comes to the fore and plays an irreplaceable role in guiding the communicators throughout the whole speech event in the processes of verbal and non-verbal interaction (Murray, 1964; Verschueren, 1999, Rostomyan, 2012). Moreover, it is generally believed that the expected actions of the trustees will not have an emotional negative impact on the *trustors* (Brown 2009), just vice versa the effects and consequences are supposed to be beneficial for both parts and have an impact on interpersonal relations (Williams, 2007).

In social communication especially there is always a certain need for *trust* because of the problem of societal complexity and contingency of events in social constellations (Quandt, 2012: 8). As everyday events cannot be fully foreseen or predicated, there is always a certain need of 'trust' between the interactants to develop safely grounded expectations upon the outcome of the events which serves a secure basis for successful social action and interaction. Hence, trust is, undoubtedly, a crucial characteristic feature of the societal communication irrespective from logical or emotional reasons, since the lack of it can result in the malfunctioning of the society. This fact leads to the observation that for the successful functioning of any cultural or sub-cultural society, there is an urgent need of trust which seems to be dwindling nowadays (Williams, 2007).

According to Quandt, there are various types of trustees: trust in people one knows quite well based on their close relationship status when the interactants possess a large amount of information on each other concerning different fields which accompanies both sides of the interlocutors during the whole speech event makes their actions mutually to a greater degree predictable, and there is trust in people whom we do not know well (Quandt, 2012).

Although a lot of scientists consider the first type of the afore-mentioned trustees as irrelevant as there is always a natural propensity in trusting in people who stand close to us, yet it has to be considered as relevant since a lot of what happens in the process of communication occurs on the basis of the communicators' background knowledge (also comprising emotional elements), which makes the joint communication possible (Ternès, Rostomyan, Gursch, Gursch, 2014).

Throughout history communication and information have been fundamental sources of over and counter-power, of domination and social change. This is because the fundamental battle being fought in society is the battle over the minds of the people. The way people think determines the fate of norms and values on which societies are constructed (Castells, 2007: 238).

According to Castells's theory, power is the structural capacity of a social actor to impose its will over other social actor(s). All institutional systems reflect power relations, as well as the limits to these power relations as negotiated by a historical process of domination and counter-domination (Castells 2007: 239). By counter-power Manuel Castells means the capacity of social actors to challenge and eventually change the power relations institutionalized in a society. According to him, in all societies, counter-power exists under different forms and with variable intensity, as one of the few natural laws of society, verified right through history, asserts that wherever domination is, there is resistance to domination, be it political, cultural, economic, psychological, or otherwise (Castels, 2007: 248).

Putman coined the term *'thin trust'* for generalized trust in alteri who are largely unknown to us – be they phenomena, persons, or institutions, which is mainly opposed to personal trust that is developed by the ego during his/her lifetime experience (Putman, 2000). Thus, these two kinds of trust are not to be viewed in opposition. Moreover, the integration and appropriate cognitive evaluation of both personal and generalized trust on the part of the *ego* can only lead to the formation of the real picture of the state of affairs (Ternès, Rostomyan, Gursch, Gursch, 2014).

In this respect it is notable that currently trust seems to be shrinking in highly developed, democratic countries. There seems to be an increasing common fear that audiences are being manipulated by the mass media, companies, services and individuals. At the same time, people in developed countries increasingly turn to alternative information sources, like social networks, various blogs and other forms of online communication where they seek for the right evaluation of the offered goods and products (Quandt, 2012: 7).

In fact, trust is an essential social and communicative notion, which is mainly aimed at a specific connection between two or more social interactants in the business sector as well.

It is essential to note that in everyday communication the concept of trust mainly depends on the social distance and interrelation of the interactants (i.e. parent – child, close friends, spouses, colleagues, mere acquaintances, strangers, etc.). In this perspective the amount of the accredited trust and the corresponding displayed emotions refers to the conception of *in-group/ out-group* people.

As can be shown in this extract taken from Mark Gimenez's book "The Colour of Law" (2007), the speakers are ingroup people as

the expressive speech act of approval and admiration is decoded correspondingly on the part of the lawyer, Mister Scott Fenney.

> *Before they had parted back at the stadium that day two weeks ago, Big Charley had said,* **"When God gives you a gift, it doesn't mean you're special. It means you're blessed."**

> *Scott finally understood what his mother had meant when she had said that he had a gift and she didn't mean football. He knew that his entire life had led him to this one moment, to this trial, to Shawanda Jones. The judge was right: She needed a hero. She needed him. And he needed her.*

> *(Gimenez, The Colour of Law, 2007: 381)*

Shawanda was an Afro-American woman, who was suspected in the murder of the chancellor's son, but de facto she was innocent. Yet as she was considered to be an out-group person at that time, nobody believed that she would be convicted as innocent. Nonetheless, Mr. Scott Fenney knew that he had the talent and ability to protect her.

Adhering to the societies norms and standards is, in fact, a very useful performance in the process of communication. Nonetheless, you have to adhere to your very own imaginations and your own standards and attitude to this or that phenomenon at hand not to contradict to yourself, which Scott Fenney did to save Shawanda's freedom and life.

According to the On-Line *"European Journal of Social Psychology"* the psychological *essentialism* perspective, people tend to explain differences between groups by attributing them different essences. Given a pervasive ethnocentrism, this tendency implies that the human essence will be restricted to the in-group whereas out-groups will receive a lesser degree of humanity. Therefore, it is argued that people attribute more uniquely human characteristics to the in-group than to the out-group (Leyens, Rodriguez-Perez et alia, 2001).

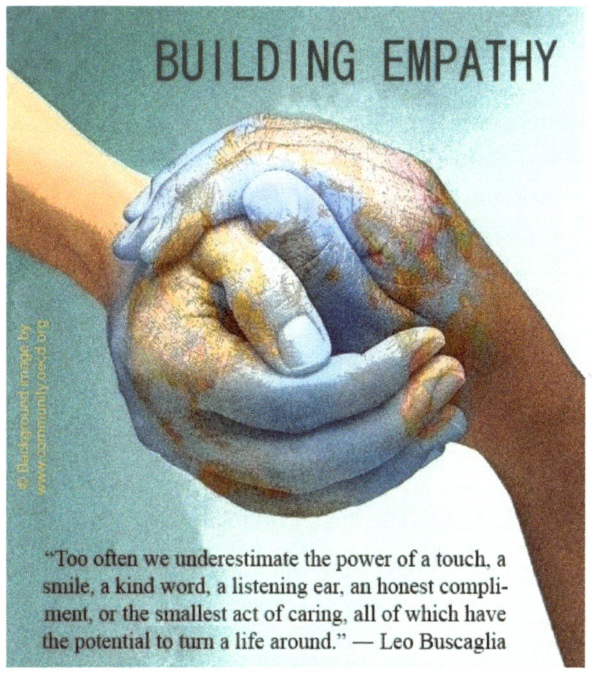

Picture 2: The Role of Empathy in Communication

Background picture source: www.community.oecd.org

Consequently, the amount of the experienced positive or negative emotions is more vital when dealing with in-group people rather than the out-group ones. This mainly depends on the fact that the brain regulates the process of expressing emotions more accurately with those who are more distant in relation with the present speaker. Hence, a very vivid emotion belonging to the scale of positive emotions comes to the fore; i.e. *empathy* and *tolerance* which may lead and contribute to a better understanding of the human nature as it may help understand the position of the opposite party and may actually direct towards the formation of a more coherent interpersonal co-operation.

Therefore, in case nowadays businessmen manage to preserve the concept of trust, virtue, and strive to handle their emerging positive and negative emotions appropriately in the process of verbal and non-verbal communication, which may have become a part of their former experiences, and ascertain trust between their interactants out of both emotional and logical reasons, which is undeniably not a very easy task indeed, they will greatly contribute to the establishment of a predictable and to a certain point controllable social order and business area.

1.3. Communication Strategies in Leading People

Communication is the keystone in leading people.

In fact, when dealing with each other verbally or non-verbally we emerge into constant flows of communication and in order to become proficient interactants, we should adhere to efficient communication techniques and strategies, which help us become more successful communicators, which resultantly will ensure better results.

According to the model of Prof. Dr. Thorsten Quandt, a Professor of Communication Studies at the University of Münster, the human societal communication system has evolved during the years and generations. The proposed schemes of communication have been thoroughly discussed by Anna and Armen Rostomyans (2018).

Finding the right words in the process of communication is not an easy task to perform. Yet, in case you are armed with the knowledge and communicative skills, you will eventually stand a better chance of having your desired emotive communicative impact on the audience.

Thus, for instance the early stage of communication processes, according to the author, looks like this, as depicted in **Diagram 1**, where we have one-to-one message transmission and receipt, which is a simple form of communication.

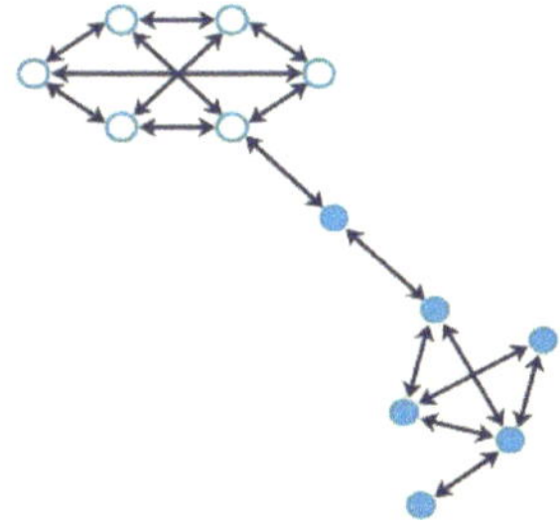

Diagram 1: Early Stage Communication (Quandt, 2012: 11)[1]

Here, we have simple societies, where people mainly interact by means of face-to-face communication; two-way communications: on one hand the encoder (speaker), on the other hand the decoder (inter-preter), it's a 1-to-1 communication where the main interactants con-stantly change roles. The communication is direct; it's interactive, syn-chronous and reactive where the main actors at hand have equal nods.

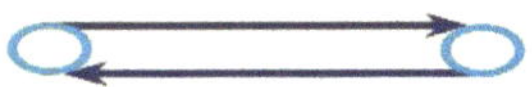

Diagram 2: one to one communication process

In the next phase we have modern societies where there is the problem of complexity of reach and distance. We can talk to people within far distances by means of technological appliances. For the infor-

---

[1] Graphic design of Diagrams 1-6 by Arman Sargsyan, BA in Arts and Design.

mation digestion and congestion, we have the selection capacity of observing and reporting which can be described as qualitative and quantitative selections.

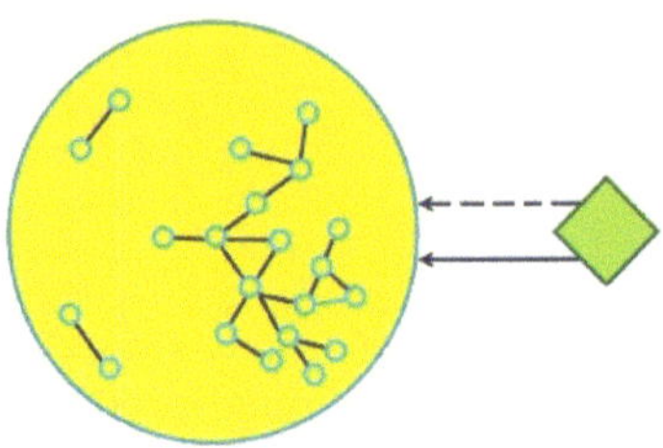

Diagram 3: Modern societies (Quandt, 2012: 12)

In this case the communication processes are selective. Communication, thus, can be described as one-way, 1-to many; it's indirect, non-reactive, unequal nods (i.e. mass audience + organizations).

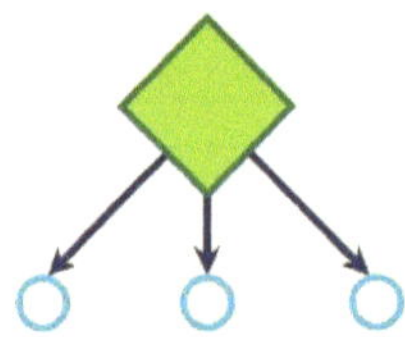

Diagram 4: Modern communication processes

Yet, it should be mentioned that in the 21st century digitalized community the societies have become really hypercomplex. (Rostomyan, A., Rostomyan, A., 2018). Media communications are all over which include millions of interactants. We should like to note that it has both advantages and shortcomings. On one hand, we get instant information, but on the other hand, it might not be safe and secure.

Firstly, one of the major assets of media communications is that messages reach their destinations within a couple of seconds. Besides, by means of diverse social networks, blogs, and personal webpages, information decoders can reach wider audiences. Nonetheless, there is a steady dilemma of misinterpretation because of complex societies which are illustrated in the diagram depicted below:

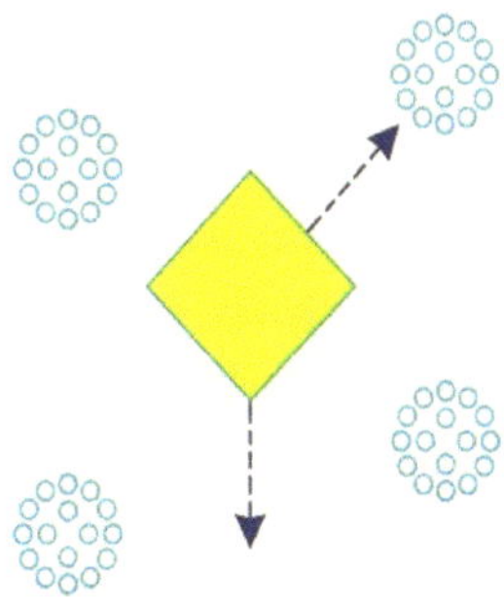

Diagram 5: Hypercomplex societies (Quandt, 2012: 12)

Here, the communication processes are very similar to the former one of modern societies with the addition of problem adaptation. In this case we have dynamics of communication due to the network system, detachment while communication and not one-to-one way of communicating, specialization of communicated topic, individualization of the decoders, sometimes disintegration because of wide social networks. In this case, there might occur diverse communication misinterpretation and misunderstandings because of the wide scope and different directions of communication.

In the hyper-complex communications communication is simultaneously directed towards multiple agents at hand, which makes it more complex and difficult to interpret.

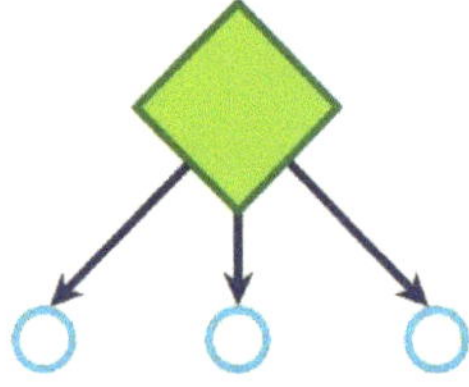

Diagram 6: Modern hypercomplex communication direction

It is noteworthy that especially in today's Business Communication, there is an urgent need of efficient communication management, taking into consideration the aforementioned strategies and communication types, particularly in terms of nowadays' remote work. Moreover, in the times of digitalization, it has become a real challenge to understand the emotions of both the employers and the employees appropriately; hence, we should take pain in properly managing our very own emotions and decoding them accordingly.

In summary, it should be noted that emotions are very prominent in leadership and in communication strategies in leading people. Factually, the analysis of the linguistic mechanisms of verbalization of emotions in the process of interpersonal communication, which has become quite urgent today, should be realized on the basis of cognitive evaluation of emotivity. The positive and negative predisposition between the interlocutors plays a vital role in the process of decoding any piece of information as well. All this also partakes in the interpretation of any piece of information. It should become your duty to strive towards managing the display of your emotions as an indispensable part of your vocation, notwithstanding ever their negative emotional disposition, which will consequently help to create a healthier working atmosphere and ensure better results.

1.4. The Nature and Psychological Aspect of Emotions and Their Expressions

We are always experiencing some sort of emotion or feeling. Our emotional state varies along the day depending on what happens to us and on the stimuli that we perceive. However, we may not always be conscious of it; that is to say, we may not know or express with clarity which emotion we are experiencing in a given moment. The experience and expression of emotions comprise a routine, yet extraordinarily complex and influential facet of the human experience, particularly in the realm of interpersonal communication.

All emotions are, in essence, impulses to act, the instant plans for handling life that evolution has instilled in us. The very root of the word emotion is "motere", the Latin verb "to move", plus the prefix "e-" to connote "move away", suggesting that a tendency to act is implicit in every emotion (Goleman, 1995: 6).

Emotions are physiological and psychological responses that *influence, perception, learning*, and *performance*. The area of emotion is complicated by the lack of general agreement on a basic definition of the nature of the concept. For example, some people take the position that emotion is an entirely different process from motivation. Others say that emotions are simply one class of motives. Some define emotion subjectively – in terms of the feeling experienced by the individual. Others see emotion as bodily changes. Most of these people have emphasized the reaction as the main component in emotion, but others concentrate on the perception of the situation that arouses the emotion or the effects of the emotion on ordinary behaviour. (James, 1890; Murray, 1964).

Generally, in our bewildering emotional repertoire we can classify the bewildering variety of emotions into two opposite poles, namely **positive** vs. **negative** emotions, which are respectively reflected in our everyday speech. The list of feelings and reactions we include under the term emotion is almost infinite. Although there may be slight differences in how positively or negatively emotions are viewed in particular situations, they tend to have reputations as being either positive or negative in general (e.g., jealousy is a "green-eyed monster"). Andersen and Guerrero even divide their book on emotions into "The 'Dark Side' of Emotions" (e.g., embarrassment, hurt, jealousy, anger, etc.) and "The 'Bright Side' of Emotions" (e.g., comforting, support, warmth, loving, etc.) (Andersen and Guerrero, 1998).

It is believed that, at birth, there are just a few basic emotional reactions that develop through learning and maturation. The behaviourist John Watson supported this viewpoint and claimed that children have three basic emotions – fear, rage and love. Subsequent studies have shown, however, that at birth emotional reactivity is even simpler than Watson believed. Observations of children, ranging in age from birth to two years, showed that initially an infant is either excited or quiescent. Stimuli of any kind elicit only the generalized excitement pattern.

Many scientists agree on diving emotions into two poles:

Negative emotions express an attempt or intention to exclude. Keeping bad stuff away, destroying what is perceived as a threat. Negative emotions are fueled by an underlying fear of the unknown, a fear of the actions of others, and a need to control them or stop them to avoid being harmed. Negative emotions are, for example: apathy, grief, fear, hatred, jealousy, rage, embarrassment, anxiety, hostility, agony, sadness, disgust, etc.

Positive emotions express an attempt or an intention to include. They help us to work on learning more viewpoints, interact easily and peacefully with others, and enjoy changing things for the better. Positive emotions are fueled by an underlying desire for enjoyment and unity. Positive emotions are, for example: joy, happiness, hilarity, bliss, love, satisfaction, amusement, delight, pleasure, desire, peace, empathy, etc. (http://www.worldtrans.org/TP/TP2/TP2A-35.HTML)

Almost invariably, a speaker's expressiveness indicates that he/she is in a heightened emotional state. Our overall investigation on the problem of emotions and the issues of intensification have drawn to the fact that in our life we cannot be only under the possession of positive and/or negative emotions, but they are most likely to follow and come into being after one another. This can also be proved by the national saying which goes like this: "After the rain there is always a rainbow", where "rain" may stand for negative emotions, and "rainbow" – for the scale of positive emotions. All in all, their intersection may be depicted like a spiral cord shown below:

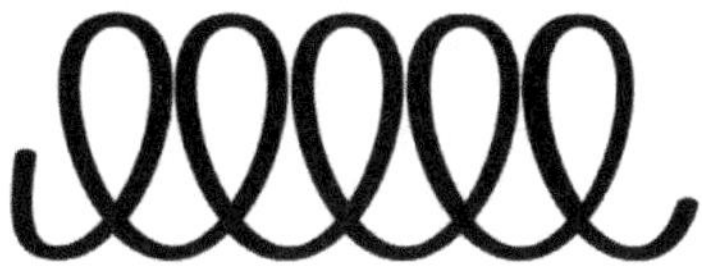

Picture 1: The Depiction of Positive and Negative Emotions as a Spiral Cord

We believe that the relationship between judgment and sensation is like an across-level spiral. At the lowest level, when an emotional subject encounters a life-affecting situation, certain specific emotional senses (such as fear or cheer) arise. Affects, turning up in fixed association with sensory perception, are epiphenomena of neurophysiological structures activated in those situations. Emotional affects are themselves believed to be judgments, because they are mutually distinct; accordingly, such affects can be referred to as emotional senses. In addition to all these processes, those senses could further serve as bases of higher-level emotional judgment, such as thinking and imagination, and, thus, the spiral goes upward. The spiral, besides, can also go downward; as a result of higher-level thinking (e.g. inference) a lower-level emotion (e.g. fear) can incur. Thus, the spiral structure of emotional sensation and judgment may allocate emotions at various levels.

It is generally believed that emotion plays the role we expect it to, i.e. communicating information about our internal states, feelings, beliefs and desires. However, in some circumstances, we observe that emotions are not demonstrated so explicitly in speech. Nonetheless, when undergoing very strong emotions the speaker will not be able to control them or to try to minimize the degree of the felt emotion, and consequently, his/her experienced emotions will be manifested in speech. Hence, in order to analyze the manifestation of emotions in speech we shall consider expressive speech acts, since whenever the parts become involved in trust, they freely make use of emotion manifestations.

There is a range of different emotions in each category as well. We could say that some are more positive or negative than others. But it isn't necessarily practical to place them on a linear scale, since each one is a composite of various elements. There are emotions that can be either positive or negative (e.g., surprise). Some emotions seem to be positive or negative, but really are the opposite of what they pretend. There is a covert hostility that masks as friendliness, which can often be difficult to assess at first. Likewise, some kinds of anger or tears might look negative, but might really be an expression of involvement and care for the whole. It is the underlying mechanism and motivation that counts, more than the superficial outward manifestation.

Having analyzed various cases of intensification, we have revealed that intensifiers can be divided into 3 groups according to nature (Rostomyan 2009):

1) *positive*: intensifiers belonging to this class reinforce the actual positive implication of the sentence by giving emotive emphasis to it, e.g.: marvelously, wondrously, fabulously, fantastically, etc., and imply the presence of positive emotions, such as: fascination, awe, love, desire, admiration, wonder, liking, and the like;

E.g.: She is a *damnably* beautifual lady!

This castle is a *wondrously* stunning architectural masterpiece!

Christian Dior's fall/winter collection is *fantastically* hot!

2) *negative*: intensifiers belonging to this class attach negative implication to the sentence by amplifying the overall negative meaning, e.g.: who/what/why/where the hell, damned/darned if, etc., and imply the presence of negative emotions, such as: resentment, frustration, embarrassment, anger, irritation, annoyance, rage, and the like;

E.g.: This apple-pie is *damn* expensive!

Who the hell do you think you are?

What the hell do you expect from me?

3) ***either positive or negative***: the nature of these intensifiers depends on the context. They can entail the presence of either positive or negative emotions depending on the context. Intensifiers of this class are: crazily, dreadfully, awfully, terribly, damn, right, pretty, too, at all, as well as many others:

E.g. She is a damnably attractive woman! – Positive
This exercise is *damnably* difficult! – Negative
This place is *pretty* cool. – Positive
They are *pretty* jealous. – Negative.

Some theorists, as Daniel Goleman, propose basic families of emotion, though not all of them agree on them. The main candidates and some of the members of their families are:

- Anger: fury, outrage, resentment, wrath, exasperation, indignation, vexation, acrimony, animosity, annoyance, irritability, hostility, and, perhaps at the extreme, pathological hatred and violence,
- Sadness: grief, sorrow, cheerlessness, gloom, melancholy, self-pity, loneliness, dejection, despair, and, when pathological, severe depression,
- Fear: anxiety, apprehension, nervousness, concern, consternation, misgiving, wariness, qualm, edginess, dread, fright, terror, as a psychopathology, phobia and panic,
- Enjoyment: happiness, joy, relief, contentment, bliss, delight, amusement, pride, sensual pleasure, thrill, rapture, gratification, satisfaction, euphoria, whimsy, ecstasy, and, at the far edge, mania,
- Love: acceptance, friendliness, trust, kindness, affinity, devotion, adoration, infatuation, agape,
- Surprise: shok, astonishment, amazement, wonder,

- Disgust: contempt, disdain, scorn, abhorrence, aversion, distaste, revulsion,
- Shame: guilt, embarrassment, chagrin, remorse, humiliation, regret, mortification, and contrition. (Goleman, 1995: 289-290)

Yet, this list is not entirely complete, since it does not include some vital emotions, such as: jealousy, faith, empathy, courage, certainty, etc. The scientific debate on how to classify emotions is still a continually ongoing and a very challenging process.

It is here noteworthy that by means of using intensification in our speech, we can very vividly display our emotions and, hence, have a positive or negative emotive impact on our listeners, which, as a matter of fact, gives us the opportunity to subtly suggesting them what emotions they should feel according to our expressed very own positive or negative emotions.

Moreover, in case we use different emotive boosters, diverse functional words called *intensifiers* in our speech, we will stand a better chance of having our desired positive or negative influence on our interlocutors; thus, subtly suggesting them what emotions they should feel. In fact, very many speakers, politicians, influencers and content writers adhere to this tiny little but effective technique to gain the emotive inclusion of their audience into the presented content. It should be mentioned that his emotional impact can be achieved for both positive and negative emotions and expressions of therein; hence, it follows that depending on the context the use of intensifiers can amplify the overall emotional content of the given speech act.

In fact, it is true that emotions are very complex experiences, and when expressing them, we use a great variety of terms, besides gestures and attitudes. In fact, as good poets show us, we could use all the words of a dictionary to express different emotions and sometimes fail to describe a specific emotion expressing all the inner shades and overtones. Therefore, due to the infinite extension of emotional phenomena, it is impossible to make a full description of all the emotions that we can experience. However, the usual vocabulary to describe emotions is quite reduced, allowing people with the same cultural background to share them. In the following **Table 1** several emotions and their corresponding description words are presented.

Positive Emotions		Negative Emotions	
I feel myself…	*I feel…*	*I feel myself…*	*I feel…*
well	well-being	uncomfortable	discomfort
happy	happiness	unfortunate	misfortune
healthy	health	sick	sickness
gay	gaiety	sad	sadness
strong	strength, etc.	weak	weakness, etc.

Table 1: The Experience of Positive and Negative Emotions

The complexity of the phenomenon makes the impression that we always lack words to describe our emotions accurately. But under this complexity, there is a common factor to all emotions: each emotion expresses a quantity or magnitude in a positive/negative scale. In this way, we experience positive and negative emotions in different degrees and with diverse intensity. We can experience abrupt or gradual changes of emotional intensity, either towards the positive or negative side. That is to say, all emotions represent a magnitude or measurement along a continuum that can take positive or negative values (Buzarov, 1969; Rostomyan, 2009).

In everyday language, we express our emotions with a positive/negative scale and in variable magnitudes with the help of different means of emotive emphasis showing degrees for positive emotions, such as in English "I feel good", "I feel *quite* good", "I feel *very* good", "I feel *absolutely* good"; in German "Ich fühle mich gut", "I fühle mich *ganz* gut", "Ich fühle mich *sehr* gut", "Ich fühle mich *hervorragend*"; in French "Je me sens bien", "Je me sens *assez* bien", "Je me sens *très* bien", "Je me sens *merveilleusement* bien"; in Russian "Я чувствую себя хорошо”, “Я чувствую себя *достаточно* хорошо”, “Я чувствую себя *очень* хорошо”, “Я чувствую себя *прекрасно*”, and finally in Armenian «Ես ինձ լավ եմ զգում», «Ես ինձ *բավականին* լավ եմ զգում», «Ես ինձ *շատ* լավ եմ զգում», «Ես ինձ *հիանալիորեն* լավ եմ զգում», and similar patterns showing degrees for negative emotions, such as in English “I feel bad”, “I feel *quite* bad”, “I feel *very* bad”, “I feel *absolutely* bad”, in German “Ich fühle mich schlecht”, “Ich fühle mich *ganz* schlecht”, “Ich fühle mich *sehr* schlecht” and “Ich fühle mich *schrecklich* schlecht”, in French “Je me sens mal”, “Je me sens *assez* mal”, “Je me sens *très* mal” and “Je me sens *terriblement* mal”, in Russian “Я себя чувствую плохо”, “Я себя чувствую *достаточно* плохо” “Я себя чувствую *очень* плохо”, , “Я себя чувствую *ужасно* плохо”, and in Armenian «Ես ինձ վատ եմ զգում», «Ես ինձ *բավականին* վատ եմ զգում», «Ես ինձ *շատ* վատ եմ զգում», «Ես ինձ *ահավոր* վատ եմ զգում» (Rostomyan, 2013b):

This can come to suggest that there is intensification playing on both the positive and negative angles of the expression of emotions under different circumstances.

According to the situation in which a certain emotion is aroused, we choose words such as “love”, “friendship”, “fear”, “uncertainty”, “respect”, etc., that, at the same time, show the emotional sign (positive or negative).

And according to the intensity of the emotion, we choose words like “quite”, “some”, “enough”, “very”, etc., and, in this way, we compose the description of an emotion. We say, for example, “I feel *very well* understood” (positive) or “I feel *a little* deceived” (negative).

As a result, we can recognize two well-differentiated components in all emotions. On one hand, there is a qualitative component that is expressed by means of the word that we use to describe the emotion (love, friendship, fear, insecurity, etc.) determining the “positiveness” or “negativeness” of the emotional sign. On the other hand, all emotions possess a quantitative component that is expressed by means of words of magnitude (little, quite, enough, a lot, great, some, much, etc.).

The following **Table 2** attempts to reflect these two components of emotions showing different degrees of emotivity.

It is noteworthy that degrees of emotivity can be expressed in speech both for expressing positive and for negative emotions.

Emotion = quantitative component + qualitative component		
Positive emotions	a little quite a lot extremely	happiness content gaity bliss
Negative emotions	a little quite a lot extremely	anger resentment rage fury

Table 2: The Magnitude of Emotions

According to the situation in which a certain emotion is aroused, we choose words such as "love", "friendship", "fear", "uncertainty", "respect", etc., that, at the same time, show the emotional sign (positive or negative). And according to the intensity of the emotion, we choose words like "quite", "awfully", "enough", "very", etc., and, in this way, we compose the description of an emotion. We say, for example, "I feel very well understood" (positive) or "I feel a little depressed" (negative). As a result, we can recognize in all emotions two well-differentiated components. On the one hand, there is a qualitative component that is expressed by means of the word that we use to describe the emotion (love, friendship, fear, insecurity, etc.) determining the "positiveness" or "negativeness" of the emotional sign. On the other hand, all emotions possess a quantitative component that is expressed by means of words of magnitude (little, quite, enough, a lot, great, some, much, etc.) (Rostomyan, 2009).

The complexity of the phenomenon makes the impression that we always lack words to describe our emotions accurately. But under this complexity, there is a common factor to all emotions: each emotion expresses a quantity or magnitude in a positive/negative scale. As we have seen, in this way, we experience positive and negative emotions in different degrees and with diverse intensity. We can experience abrupt or gradual changes of emotional intensity, either towards the positive or negative side. That is to say, all emotions represent a magnitude or measurement along a continuum that can take positive or negative values. Thus, in everyday language, we express our emotions with a positive/negative scale and in variable magnitudes with the help of different means of emotive emphasis, such as "I feel good" "I feel *quite* good", "I feel *very* good" (showing degrees for positive emotions) or "I feel bad", "I feel *quite* bad", "I feel *very* bad" (showing degrees for negative emotions) (Rostomyan, 2009).

As we know, we can express our emotions through certain gestures, movements or facial expressions. But it is also obvious that our inner world is basically reflected in our speech. The reason why we choose to use a particular expression or certain grammatical pattern is mainly to be found in our state of mind, our mood, that is to say it greatly depends on the emotion we experience on the very moment of the act of communication (Lee and Narayanan, 2005).

Thus, both in everyday communication and in business communication, we make use of very different means expressing our positive and negative emotions and means of expressing. We are inclined to adhere to the viewpoint that the wide range of emotions and emotional states can be classified into positive and negative poles.

Another important factor that should by all means be taken into account is facial expression. Let us see which particular facial expression we display undergoing this or that emotion. As already mentioned, neither emotions, nor their expressions are concepts universally embraced by psychologists. The term "expression" implies the existence of something that is expressed. Some psychologists deny that there is really any specific organic state that corresponds to our naive ideas about human emotions. Other psychologists think that the behaviours referenced by the term "expression" are part of an organized emotional response, and thus, the term "expression" captures these behaviours' role less adequately than a reference to it as an aspect of the emotion reaction. Still others think that facial expressions have primarily a communicative function and convey something about intentions or internal state, and they find the connotation of the term "expression" useful (Murray, 1964).

Research shows that people categorize emotion faces in a similar way across cultures, that similar facial expressions tend to occur in response to particular emotion eliciting events, and that people produce simulations of emotion faces that are characteristic of each specific emotion (Ekman, 1972, 1975, 2004).

Despite some unsettled theoretical implications of these findings, a consensus view is that in studies of human emotions, it is often useful to know what facial expressions correspond to each specific emotion, and the answer is summarized briefly below:

Happy expressions are universally and easily recognized, and are inter-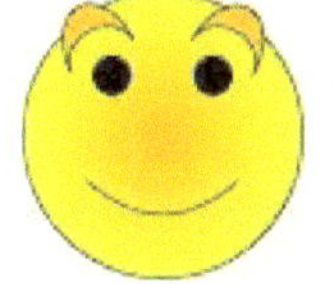preted as conveying messages related to enjoyment, pleasure, a positive disposition, and friendliness. Smile is the most commonly indicator of happiness across cultures. In fact, happy expressions may be practiced behaviours because they are used so often to hide other emotions and deceive or manipulate other people. This can be well illustrated by bringing the example of invariably smiling political figures and other celebrities on television.

Sad expressions are often conceived as opposite to happy ones. Sad ex-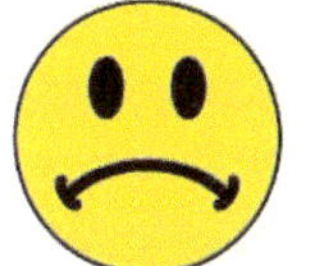pressions convey messages related to loss, discomfort, pain, helplessness, etc. A common-sense view, shared by many psychologists, is that sad emotion faces are lower intensity forms of crying faces. The main expression of a sad facial expression is the mouth lowered a bit at the corners. Although weeping and tears are a common concomitant of sad expressions, tears are not indicative of any particular emotion, as in tears of joy.

Anger expressions are seen increasingly often in modern society, as 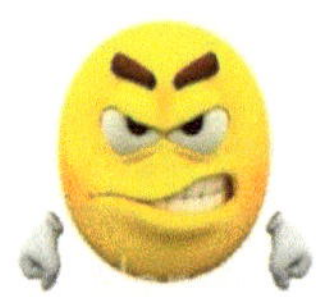 daily stresses, depressions, and frustrations underlying anger seem to increase. Anger is a primary concomitant of interpersonal aggression, and its expression conveys messages about hostility, opposition, and potential attack. The uncontrolled expression of rage exerts a toxic effect on the angry person, and chronic anger seems associated with certain patterns of behaviour that correspond to unhealthy outcomes. The main indicators of anger are the "wrapped" eyebrows and clutched feasts. Although frequently associated with violence and destruction, anger is probably the most socially constructive emotion as it often underlies the efforts of individuals to shape societies into better environments, and to resist the imposition of injustice and tyranny.

Fear expressions are not often seen in societies where good personal  security is typical, because the imminent possibility of personal destruction, from interpersonal violence or impersonal dangers, is the primary elicitor of fear. Fear expressions are mostly manifested by widely opened eyes and they usually convey information about imminent danger, a nearby threat, a disposition to flee, or likelihood of bodily harm. Anxiety is related to fear, and may involve some of the same bodily responses, but is a longer-term mood and the elicitors are not as immediate. Both are associated with unhealthy physical effects if prolonged.

Disgust expressions are often part of the body's responses to objects 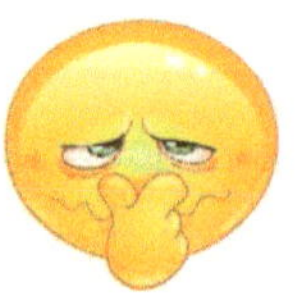 that are revolting and nauseating, such as rotting flesh, insects in food, or other offensive materials that are rejected as suitable to eat. Detestable smells are effective in eliciting disgust reactions.

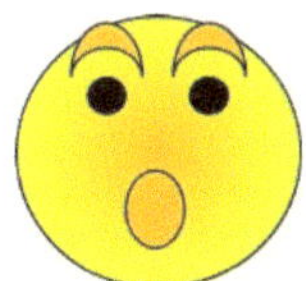

Surprise expressions are fleeting, and difficult to detect or record in real time. They almost always occur in response to events that are unanticipated, and they convey messages about something being unexpected, sudden, novel, or amazing. The brief surprise expression is often followed by other expressions that reveal emotion in response to the surprise feeling or to the object of surprise, emotions such as happiness or fear. For example, most of us have been surprised, perhaps intentionally, by people who appear suddenly or do something unexpected, and thus elicit surprise; if the person is a friend, a typical after-emotion is happiness; if you are encountered with a stranger, the resulting emotion is typically fear.

(http://face-and-emotion.com/dataface/emotion/expression.jsp)

The question to what extent facial expressions are innately related to emotion is still under consideration and requires further investigation and study. One thing is obvious that children who are deaf and blind tend to show the same expressions in the same situations at about the same age as normal children. This suggests innate patterns. At the same time, undoubtedly social learning has some effect on the way emotions are expressed facially too. For example, lots of diverse nations like the Armenians, Russians, Germans, Americans, etc. express surprise by raising the eyebrows, whereas the Chinese stick out their tongues in the same situation.

It is as well noteworthy that in the complex process of communication we do not only make use of phonological, morphological, grammatical or syntactic rules, but we also take into consideration the social roles of the interlocutors, they relationship distance, their positive or negative emotional predisposition towards one another, etc. That is to say much of what we say and a great deal of what we communicate is determined by our social relationships. In fact, every act of interpersonal communication, including emotional expression in communication, occurs within a social context. Discussing the importance of social relationships and the corresponding roles, Hartley asserts:

"Any communication between two people will be influenced by the relationship which exists between them. This relationship can be of different types which reflect different roles (e.g., friend, brother) and of different quality (e.g., close and informal as opposed to distant and formal). . . Every social situation incorporates some definition of the roles that are expected of the participants. And these expected roles influence how and what people will communicate."

(Hartley 1993: 90)

Whether referred to as relationship level, role relationship, or target characteristics, aspects relevant to targets of an interaction play an important part in any examination of interpersonal phenomena, specifically within the area of emotion as the appropriateness of any emotional display may greatly depend on the target. We may here quote George Yule, who asserts: "A linguistic interaction is necessarily a social interaction" (Yule 1996: 59).

In case we are aware of the verbal and non-verbal emotion expressions, we will consequently be more self-aware and will accordingly respond to outward situations, which will add to our emotional intelligence and will help us in our self-management in building long-lasting relationships.

1.5.   Pragmatics and Speech Acts

Pragmatics or otherwise called **Pragmalinguistics** is a subfield of linguistics and semiotics that studies the ways in which context contributes to meaning. Pragmatics encompasses speech act theory, conversational implicature, talk in interaction and other approaches to language behavior in philosophy, sociology, linguistics and anthropology. Pragmatics studies how we can do things via language having our desired emotive impact on the audience on the perlocutionary level.

When discussing the problem of successful Business Communication, it should by all means be viewed from a pragmalinguistic perspective as well, since far too much of what happens in the process of business interaction, occurs on the communicative level.

In fact, when uttering a sentence, the speaker is simultaneously performing three speech acts: **locutionary**, **illocutionary** and **perlocutionary**, which are the basis of pragmatic analysis.

The *locutionary* level is what one says (e.g. I feel cold); the *illocutionary* level is what one implies by saying that (e.g. Please, light the fire or give me a blanket), the *perlocutionary* level is the illocutionary effect on the interlocutor (e.g. you, being the interlocutor urged to do something for the sake of the person who says that he/she is cold) (Yule, 1996; Levison, 1983).

The illocutionary component of a speech act lies in what the utterance does rather than what it says. There are different illocutionary force indicating devices, for example word order, stress, and intonation (punctuation), the mood of the verb, context, etc. Speech acts may be classified into six groups: **declarations**, **representatives**, **expressives**, **directives**, **commissives**, and **questions**. Illocutionary acts are valid only in case their felicity conditions are met.

In pragmatics, an utterance needs to be felicitous to be considered valid; thus, it has to meet the felicity conditions. Felicity condition underlies that in order to be felicitous, an utterance must meet the felicity conditions that include *preparatory condition, propositional content, sincerity condition,* and *essential condition* (Austin, 1962; Searle, 1969; Levinson, 1983; Yule, 1996). In case one of the aforementioned felicity conditions is violated, for instance, the felicity condition of sincerity, an utterance can be decoded in a different light of thought.

To understand communication better, we have to have an understanding of different speech acts and their description.

Speech Act Classification:

Declarations are those kinds of speech acts that change the world via their utterance:

E.g.: Priest: *I hereby pronounce you husband and wife.*
Judge: *We find the defendant guilty.*

Representatives are those kinds of speech acts that state what the speaker believes to be the case or not. E.g.: *The Earth is flat. The Moon goes round the Earth. The Earth goes round the Sun.*

Expressives are those kinds of speech acts that state what the speaker feels. They express psychological states and can be statements of pleasure, pain, likes, dislikes, joy, or sorrow.

E.g.: *I'm awfully sorry! Congratulations! I feel very lucky!*
Thank you very much! My deepest thanks to you!

Directives are those kinds of speech acts that speakers use to get someone else to do something.

E.g.: *Give me a cup of tea, please. Make it black! Put a lemon in it! Don't touch that! Don't go out! Do your homework!*

Commissives are those kinds of speech acts that speakers use to commit themselves to some future action. They express what the speaker intends.

E.g.: *I'll be back. I'm going to make it right the next time.*
I promise to be back at 5 o'clock. I'll take care of you.
(Yule 1996: 53-54)

Questions are those kinds of speech acts with the help of which one may get the other do something by asking politely or asking for permission to do something.

E.g.: *Can you pass the salt, please? May I open the window?*

In this case, we can observe direct and indirect speech acts: we can perform a directive speech act by means of a question, which in this can will be understood as an indirect request.

Hence, **illocutionary acts** can be achieved either through an explicit or non-explicit performative, which in its turn is either direct or indirect as shown in **Diagram 7**:

ILLOCUTIONARY ACT

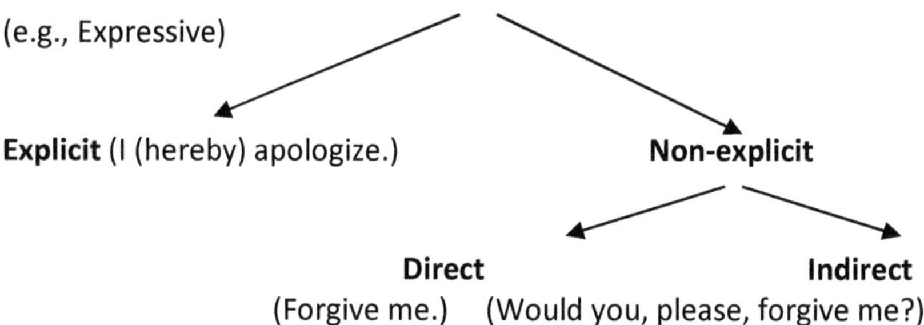

Diagram 7: The Illustration of the Illocutionary Act Diagram

A Speaker can mean just what he says, or he can mean something more or something else entirely. Grice's theory of *conversational implicature* aims to explain how this happens. For example, by stating "There is a garage around the corner," one can tell someone where to get gas, or the "Mr. X's command of English is excellent, and his attendance has been regular," can be used to state (indirectly) that Mr. X is well-qualified. These are all examples in which what is meant is not determined by what is said.

Grice proposed several maxims which he named, in homage to Kant, **Quantity**, **Quality**, **Relation**, and **Manner** (Kant's Modality). As he formulates them, they enjoin one to speak truthfully, informatively, relevantly, perspicuously, and otherwise appropriately. His account of implicature explains how ostensible violations of them can still lead to communicative success. The description of each maxim according to Yule (1996) is given below:

Quantity
1. Make your contribution as informative as is required (for the current purposes of the exchange.
2. do not make your contribution more informative than is required.

Quality – Try to make your contribution one that is true.
1.   Do not say what you believe to be false.
2.   Do not say that for which you lack adequate evidence.

Relation – Be relevant

Manner – Be perspicuous
1.   Avoid obscurity of expression.
2.   Avoid ambiguity.
3.   Be brief (avoid unnecessary prolixity).
4.   Be orderly (George Yule, 1996: 37).

Although Grice presents them as guidelines for how to communicate successfully, we know that very often the speaker deliberately flouts this or that maxim, or even flouts a combination of maxims. The listener presumes that the speaker is being cooperative and is speaking truthfully, informatively, relevantly, perspicuously, and otherwise appropriately. If an utterance superficially appears not to match this presumption, the listener looks for a way of taking the utterance so that it does conform. He does so partly on the supposition that he is intended to (Grice 1969, 1975).

The speaker takes advantage of this in choosing his words to make evident his communicative intention. Because of their potential clashes, these maxims or presumptions should not be viewed as comprising a decision procedure. Rather, they provide different dimensions of considerations that the speaker may reasonably intend that the hearer takes into account to figure out the speaker's communicative intention. Exploiting these presumptions, a speaker can say one thing and manage to mean something else or means something more. The listener relies on these presumptions to make a contextually driven inference from what the speaker says to what he means.

These maxims or presumptions do not concern what to convey at a given stage of a conversation (unless information of a very specific sort is required, say in answer to a question, there will always be lots of good ways to contribute a conversation). Rather, they frame how as listeners we are to figure out what the speaker is trying to convey by the sentence he is uttering and what he is saying in uttering it. Our job is to determine what he could have been trying to convey. Why did he say 'believe' rather than 'know', 'is' rather than 'seems', 'soon' rather than 'in an hour', 'warm' rather than 'hot', 'has the ability to' rather than 'can'?

Grice's notion of implicature can be extended to illocutionary acts. A single utterance may be the performance of one illocutionary act by way of performing another. For example, we can make a request or give permission by way of making a statement, say by uttering "It's getting cold in here" or "I don't mind," and we can make a statement or give an order by way of asking a question, such as "Can you open the door?" When an illocutionary act is performed indirectly, it is performed by way of performing some other one directly. This is mainly performed on the basis of ***mutual knowledge***/ common knowledge/ common ground/ background information/ background assumptions. Similarly, in the case of the following exchange of thoughts:

A: *What time is it?*

B: *The postman has come.*

These two people have the same background knowledge. It can be that they are neighbours or colleagues, and when B says that the postman has come, both of them know that there is an exact time for the milkman to arrive, and A decodes the given information accordingly.

Besides, the force or the content of the illocutionary act being performed is not the one that would be predicted just from the meaning of the words being used. Occasionally utterances are both nonliteral and indirect. For example, one might utter "*I love the sound of your voice*" to tell someone nonliterally (ironically) that he/she can't stand the sound of somebody's voice and thereby indirectly to ask him to stop singing.

Grice leaves the impression that the distinction between what is said and what is implicated is exhaustive (he counted irony, metaphor, and other kinds of figurative utterances as cases of implicature), but there is a common phenomenon that Grice seems to have over-looked. There are many sentences whose standard uses are not strictly determined by their meanings but are not oblique (implicature-producing) or figurative uses either. For example, if one's spouse says "I will be home later" she is likely to mean that she will be home later that night, not merely at some time in the future. Or suppose your child comes crying to you with a minor injury and you say to him in an assuring manner: *"You're not going to die."* You don't mean that he will never die but merely that he won't die from that injury. In both cases you do not mean precisely what you are saying but something more specific. In such cases what one means is what may be called an expansion of what one says, in that adding more words ('tonight' or 'from that injury', in the examples) would have made what was meant fully explicit. In other cases, such as 'Jack is ready' and 'Jill is late', the sentence does not express a complete proposition. There must be something which Jack is being claimed to be ready for and something which Jill is being claimed to be late to. In these cases what one means is a completion of what one says. In both cases, no particular word or phrase is being used nonliterally and there is no indirection. Both exemplify conversational implicature, since part of what is meant is communicated not explicitly but implicitly, by way of expansion or completion.

In implicature the speaker means something that goes beyond sentence meaning without necessarily implicating anything or using any expressions figuratively. Utterances like *"You're not going to die"* may be described as cases of sentence nonliterality, because the words are being used literally but the sentence as a whole is being used loosely. We can compare the sentence mentioned above with the following sentence: "Everybody is going to die," which would likely be used in a strictly literal way.

To sum up, emotions and their expressions are generally classified according to the positive/negative scale. Business Communication takes a vital interest in and great usage of Pragmatics, which is a branch of linguistics, as a means of social action and interaction on the basis of a special system of rules, speech acts, felicity conditions, and maxims.

In conclusion, business environment rapidly grows digitalized, where human communication become of utmost importance in interpersonal relations; namely, human communication, which is not devoid of diverse feelings and strong emotions, which find their actual verbal and non-verbal manifestations not only in everyday life situation, but also in the business environment. This section gave an overview of the important general questions on communication strategies and emotion displays, which can be applied and found in everyday speech. Hence, it should be brought home not only employers, but also employees to be aware of their very own emotions, as well as the emotions of the others, their colleagues, subordinates, and employees, and, consequently, applying their knowledge and EQ, try to understand their needs in order to be able to build a strong empire which is both successful and healthy at the same time. For this very reason, they need to be aware of successful communication strategies and emotion management techniques, which can be applied to build strong interpersonal relations, and which will be thoroughly discussed in the next section in our further chapters.

Section Two

Passion and Reason

1.4. The Role of Emotions in Business Management

Largely speaking, Business Communication is generally goal-oriented; it aims at establishing peaceful relations with the colleagues and transmitting and receiving information. Business environment, indeed, increasingly grows very complex where human resources become the only sustainable source of competitive advantage for any Management. In terms of today's capitalized and globalized world, it has become the challenge of each and every manager and entrepreneur to increase the turnover and motivation for the qualitative employees to stay and work the best way they can for their companies' targets. All these cannot be performed unless the manager is well aware of his/her employees' abilities, potential, needs and expectancies. Still, there is also a great factor that should by all means be taken into consideration, namely emotions. Being a motivator, a leader, a listener, a moderator and a presenter, the manager should at the same time take the role of a psychologist processing the information on his employees' emotions, feelings, beliefs and desires, which will eventually ensure a better understanding of their own selves and will guarantee preservation of interpersonal good and stable relations, which in their turn will eventually ensure better results and larger labour output in your business.

A professional manager should by all means be able to communicate amicably with the employees so that they, first of all, feel positive disposition towards them, unless there is no proper reason to spoil their harmonious relations. Actually, it is generally known that communication and discussion mainly rely on the interpretive power of the speakers; this is the reason why a large portion of information is being conveyed through speech implicitly – without saying it openly. Leadership, in particular, is necessarily linked with the ability of interpretation and processing of information. In fact, in the process of communication far too much is based on the emotional level, i.e. the positive or negative emotions of the speakers and their emotional background knowledge which, as a matter of fact, can frame resultant positive or negative disposition between the interactants. To understand the most vital issues connected with the personnel communicative relations we first of all need to penetrate into the interesting, as well as challenging field of emotional speech which can be carried out only after having a precise and accurate understanding of what communication generally and emotional background knowledge in particular are, viewing the problem at hand both from the local and the cross-cultural angles (Rostomyan, 2012).

Communication actually is mainly being treated as a process, which is largely based on the mental world of the speakers and embraces a great deal of conscious and subconscious framework. Models to describe this are familiar in linguistics as models of speech acts as Schulz von Thun describes it with his suggestion of four sides of a message. He proposed the communication model called a "four-side model" which is also known as "communication square" or "four-ears model". According to this model every piece of information includes four messages. The four sides of the information are fact, self-revealing, relationship, and appeal (Friedemann Schulz von Thun, 1981). The communication square describes the multi-layered structure of human utterance. It combines the postulate (second axiom) of Paul Watzlawick (Watzlawick, P., Beavin, J. H., Jackson, D. D., 1969) which implies that every communication has content and relationship aspect, with the three sides of the Organon model proposed by Karl Bühler, according to which every piece of information contains something about the matter, the sender and the receiver (Bühler, 1999).

Discourse analysts hold that the mental, social and physical realities "get 'activated' by the utterer and the interpreter in their respective choice-making practices, and that is how they become part of language use as elements with which the making of choices is interadaptable." (Verschueren, 1999: 88). It is of common ground that in the process of communication we do not always communicate with each other in an explicit manner and very often a lot of things are mutually understood by the speakers without saying them openly (Searle, 1975; Levinson 1983; Friedemann Schulz von Thun, Johannes Ruppel et alia, 2000/2003).

Interpersonal communication, in fact, is not only based on conveying, receiving, and processing information, but also expressing our internal feelings and emotions. Actually, emotions can be communicated through verbal and non-verbal means of communication, i.e. facial expressions, gross bodily movements, gestures, etc. As for the verbalization of emotions in the process of communication, there exist certain function words called *intensifiers*, such as very, pretty, awfully, immensely, tremendously, etc., which are used to modify or intensify the whole sentence or only part of it and, particularly, the emotional content.

It should be mentioned that when experiencing this or that emotion, people often tend to display that very emotion in an exaggerated manner, more strongly than they actually feel it so that to achieve their desired effect on the interlocutor. On the other hand, there are also some cases when they try to hide the experienced emotion in order to give an impression that the emotion is felt less strongly than it is in reality, or just by making their speech less firm, leave some space for doubt. These are considered to be two opposite emotion management techniques: *intensification* and *de-intensification*; which will be minutely discussed in the present book. We shall examine both the maximizing and minimizing means of the categoricity of the statement. This strategy will enable us to have a clear-cut idea of either pole. Thus, focusing on intensifiers giving emotive force to certain parts of the sentence, we shall try to find the most common intensifiers which truly reflect emotions expressed in everyday speech and group them according to their nature and to the part of the sentence they are attached to.

It is generally believed that emotion plays the role we expect, i.e. to communicate information about our internal states, feelings, beliefs, desires. However, in some circumstances, emotions are not demonstrated explicitly in speech. Nonetheless, when undergoing very strong emotions, the speakers are not able to control the display of the felt emotion or to try to minimize the degree of it, and consequently, the experienced emotions are manifested in speech with the help of verbal and non-verbal signs. Moreover, sometimes people tend to display this or that emotion in a more exaggerated manner to have their desired emotional impact on the interlocutors. Besides, there are some cases when they try to hide or reduce the degree of intensity of the experienced emotion to give an impression that the emotion is felt less strongly than it is in reality, or just by making their speech less firm, leave some space for further speculations. In fact, it is notable that in everyday life individuals sometimes do intensify or suppress the expression of emotions for certain self-presentational goals.

The linguistic expression of emotions has to do with pragmalinguistic approach to language phenomena, since albeit emotions may be expressed in gross bodily movements and facial expressions; one's emotional state is basically expressed in speech. It is also noteworthy that emotions not only reflect the speaker's emotional state, but also his/her intention, communicative goal, which naturally deals with the perlocutionary level of the speech act. Of course, there are instances of honest communication in which people make no effort to control the emotional messages they send; however, in everyday communication we often witness people trying to use different means of modifying the appearance and expression of their emotional experience.

To finalize, much has been said so far about aspects of implicit meaning in Pragmatics by many outstanding linguists, such as Searle, Grice, Yule, Levinson, Verschueren, van Dijk and many others. Research carried out in this field of analysis comes to prove that speakers usually exercise their interpretative power to decode the illocutionary force of the speech act, to guess the implicature hidden in the message, to grasp the effect of irony or sarcasm in speech, to recognize the clichéd behavioural frames and practice the scenarios stored in the long-term memory in order to decode the strategic involvement of the particular speech event, and so on. Undoubtedly, the role of background emotional memory in the process of communicative interaction is of utmost importance. In fact, a skilled manager should be aware of the role of emotional background knowledge between the interactants and should seek for ways to implement emotion management techniques to avoid communicative conflict between the employer and the employees.

2.2.   The Urgency of Emotion Expression Management

As we have given stated, our human communication not only consists in coding and decoding information, but also conveying our inner states, feelings, thoughts, beliefs, wishes and desires, which all in all are usually encoded through verbal and non-verbal means of communication. Everyday life actually progresses in the form of regular interactions with our potential social partners – relatives, friends, colleagues whom we encounter on various social occasions. Our human nature incorporates a great variety of factors which altogether shape our behaviour, and emotions also greatly partake in the formation of the general framework of the communicative context. No doubt the ability to converse, to share our thoughts and feelings with other members of the public has been originally encoded in such a way that speakers should have a positive predisposition to their social co-partners, however depending on various factors, subjective or objective, people sometimes spoil their harmonious relations, which very often occurs because of speech conflicts.

Communication, in general, is subconsciously inclined towards mutual understanding and respect. It normally aims at building a cohesive, unified, tolerant society and establishing peaceful relations with the members of the given speech community. Thus, speakers should usually have an innate predisposition to communicate amicably, unless there is some reason for them to ruin up their harmonious public relations by arguing, disputing, debating and quarrelling with each other. As a matter of fact, whenever we are emotionally upset, we are very often more inclined to misinterpret the decoded messages, attaching extra negative emotive emphasis to them; on the contrary, positive emotions usually lead us into positive evaluations, sympathetic disposition and mutual understanding (Paronyan, Rostomyan, 2011b: 7-14).

Undoubtedly, the exceptional importance of emotions in human life has already been a crucial subject matter both in linguistics and in some social sciences (such as neurolinguistics, psycholinguistics, cognitive psychology, cognitive linguistics, pragmalinguistics, sociology, sociolinguistics, social psychology, etc.). The analyses of verbal behaviour, which proceeds in the form of negative emotional colouring and results in conflict talk, illustrate the major role of the emotional mind (the speakers' diverse emotions and feelings, thoughts, beliefs, desires and wishes, motivations and intentions) in shaping the communicative context. No doubt, the involvement of the negative emotional attitude of the interlocutors in the process of communication, particularly in the realm of personnel relations, becomes evident in terms of production and interpretation of speech, which actually negatively affects the overall labour output and causes consequential tense relations between the interactants.

As we can see, the field of emotions itself is very complex, fascinating, as well as quite challenging when one tries to reveal the nature of human emotiveness, to penetrate into the inner world of the speakers and to examine how this or that very emotion is manifested in linguistic behaviour. As a matter of fact, being humans, we always experience some sort of emotion or feeling. Moreover, our emotional state varies throughout the day depending on the external stimuli that we perceive. Truly, interpersonal communication is highly influenced by the interlocutors' inner world, their feelings and emotions, beliefs and desires, as well as positive or negative predisposition towards each other (Paronyan, Rostomyan, 2011b; Rostomyan, 2012).

It is also noteworthy that while communicating with each other we are always restricted by diverse predefined *display rules* set by this or that society, which are referred to as guidelines for *when, where* and *how* to appropriately manage the display of an emotion and which may naturally vary across cultures (Rostomyan, 2013a,b). As a matter of fact, *display rules* are learnt so early in life that they become habitual later on. They provide people with expectations about how others should act and react so that social interaction could become to some extent predictable. Backman claims that this common ground among people *'makes the joint construction of reality and action in concert possible'* (Backman 1985, 272). Camras explains that (Camras, 1985: 153):

> *"...communication of emotion via choice of language could be particularly important in situations where display rules militate against the use of emotional facial expressions."*

While observing the nature of the expression and management of emotions Ekman and Friesen propose four sources of display rules: 1) *cultural display rules*, 2) *personal display rules*, 3) *vocational requirements*, and 4) *need of the moment* (Ekman and Friesen, 1975).

Cultural display rules are the conventions *'followed by all (non-rebellious) members of a given social class, sub-culture, or culture'* (Ekman 1975, 138). Examples of cultural display rules comprise instances of exhibiting grief at funerals, displaying joy at weddings and birthdays, men not exhibiting fear or tears in public, or women not exhibiting anger in public. It is notable that some nations are generally considered to be more inclined to handle their emotions whereas others rarely tend to suppress them.

Moreover, Malatesta and Izard explain that in Western cultures many display rules (Malatesta and Izard 1984: 4):

> *'...are directed at augmenting the more social, sanguine emotional expressions (smiling, interest, empathy) and exhibiting or muting those with potential to escalate benign interaction into conflict encounters (anger, jealousy, contempt) or those with potential to disturb others through contagion (sadness, anxiety).'*

Besides, Ekman and Friesen (1975) suggest that, in fact, the so-called *sub-cultures* develop and sustain their own specific characteristic display rules. These rules may change in due course of time, circumstances (e.g., the presence of children, the presence of unfamiliar people, etc.), or according to the level of relationship (e.g., close friends, married couples, employer-employee, parent-infant, etc.). It should be noted that individuals may also differ in the way they adhere to and manifest cultural display rules. In other words, some people may be more likely to intensify emotions across cultures and situations, whereas others may generally be more inclined to suppress them irrespective of the current circumstances. This phenomenon leads to the observation that besides cultural display rules there are personal display rules which can also be detected in interpersonal communication.

Personal display rules are generally considered to stem from families. Matsumoto speaks about the existence of such personal display rules, suggesting that different families *'may allow the expression of certain emotions but not others'* (Matsumoto, 1991: 131). Consequently, it is considered that family predefined display rules which solidify in maturity might encourage overt displays of anger, resentment or aggression, and suppression of excitement, amusement or joy, irrespective of the general culturally governed display rules.

The third influential component that has an impact on the expression management of emotions is the **vocational requirements**. In this group we consider people who have to act in certain ways according to their profession. Many jobs require what Hochschild calls an *emotional labour* (Hochschild, 1983: 95). His use of this concept involves flight attendants who, because of the demands of their occupation, engage in surface and deep structures of acting in order to shape the outward appearance of a tranquil, unworried, distressed, relaxed and pleasant emotional state. For instance, the employees of a bank have to manage their emotions and when dealing with their customers in conflict situations by no means let their emotions govern their behaviour, without explicitly demonstrating the felt negative emotions in speech. Likewise, during presidential debates the candidates do not display their irritation or negative disposition towards one another. In fact, politicians, doctors, teachers/lecturers, lawyers, economists, as well as other specialists can be included in the category of those who have to control their emotions as a part of their vocations.

Finally, Ekman and Friesen (1975) suggest that the **need of the moment** greatly influences emotion expression and emotion management as well. This proposed group includes examples of controlling the expression of emotions for a certain personal gain, e.g. a guilty criminal who lies displaying a seemingly innocent face when pleading guiltless to have an impact on the jurors and the Judge. While these may seem congruent with general culturally-governed display rules, the authors view such incidents of emotion management as a distinct kind (Rostomyan, 2012).

Summarizing the aforementioned four types of display rules, we reveal that all of them are intended to identify stereotyped rules according to which people have to display or to manage their emotions depending on the circumstances which may naturally vary across cultures, sub-cultures, individuals, and situations. Yet, it should be born in mind that over-suppression of emotions may also be destructive, thus, one should find the golden middle of balancing and inhibiting emotions. All this comes to prove that emotion management and accurate emotional labour should become a part-and-parcel of the lives of both the employers and the employees.

2.3. The Role of Background Knowledge in Communication

Our human nature incorporates a rich variety of factors which shape our behaviour in general. Being a specific form of social behaviour, speech is based on a number of essential features forming the general framework of the communicative context where the role of background knowledge gains utmost importance.

Recent research work carried out within the frames of Discourse Analysis and Cognitive Linguistics comes to prove the essential importance of mental activities in our linguistic behaviour.

Communication is treated as a process which is largely based on the mental world of the speakers and embraces a great deal of conscious and subconscious framework.

According to William James, each personality has a verified spectrum of his own "identity" and his own "self". The renowned psychologist claims that we have our *"biological self"*, *"real self"*, *"social self"*, and *"spiritual self"*, which are closely intertwined (James, 1890). All these "selves" are interconnected by one's memory which in its turn can be **rational** or **emotional**.

The term **'emotional memory'** was introduced into cognitive linguistics not a very long time ago (Murray, 1964). This term comes to show how two important aspects of human mind – emotion and memory – are interrelated. Emotional memory forms an essential part of the situational context in terms of the cognitive-pragmatic aspect of discursive behaviour (Paronyan, Rostomyan, 2011a, 2011b; Rostomyan, 2012). It provides a reliable basis for the successful function of the components of background knowledge. Background knowledge (also called common knowledge, mutual knowledge) refers to various aspects of the communicative context – the physical world or the immediate environment in which communication is maintained, the social world or the social factors of the interlocutors (their age, status, intimacy, etc.) and, finally, the mental world.

The aspect of background knowledge that belongs to the mental world contains both rational and emotional elements. Hence, the mental world contains chunks of knowledge of the objective world which are stored in the memory in the form of scenarios and strategic frames as any perception is almost always a subjective one. Furthermore, the mental world is connected with human psychology and is built out of our former emotional experiences, as well as our further perception and cogitation of the latters; that is, it depends to a certain extent on the psychological characteristics of the interlocutors – their emotional experiences, socialization, expectations, intentions, and dispositions of the speakers in the process of communication (Paronyan, Rostomyan, 2011: 7-14).

We are always experiencing some sort of emotion or feel even without being conscious about it. Our decisions and interpersonal relations are, in fact, very often influenced by our past emotional experiences, which are stored in our emotional background knowledge.

The results of an empiric survey carried out by us which are displayed in **Chart 1** presented below come to suggest that negative emotional experiences are stored in the long-term memory, cling to it more intensely and have a negative influence on interpersonal relations in a more enhanced manner than positive emotions. As a result, 63 percent of the 100 people interviewed demonstrated the intensity and impact of enhanced negative emotional memory; while only 37 percent of them claimed and displayed that positive emotions can also be reserved and stored in the emotional mind, consequently having a positive impact on interpersonal relations as illustrated in **Chart 1**:

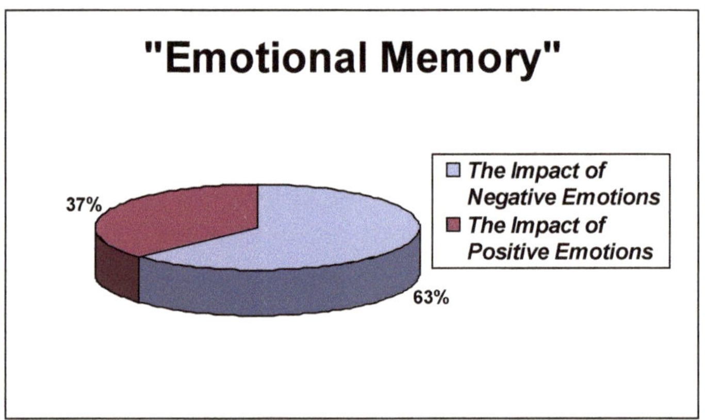

Chart 1: The Ratio of the Impact of Positive and Negative Emotions

(Chart source: Rostomyan, 2012: 285)

These indexicals of the psychological state of the interlocutors at the moment of speech production predetermine the emotive charge of speech (both explicit and implicit) – attach emotional effect to speech, make an emotional and logical impact on the hearer and, simultaneously, form a basis for the hearer to interpret the speech act emotionally. Hence, emotional memory works both for the speaker, who encodes certain emotive positive or negative meaning according to some former emotional experiences, and the interpreter, who correspondingly decodes the speaker's intended meaning emotively. Thus, we assume that a large part of implicit meaning, which remains unsaid and veiled in the process of interaction, is truly related to human emotions and feelings. The speakers' past negative or positive emotional experience, which, as we have given stated, is also part of mutually shared background knowledge, determines the choice of certain language data on a particular occasion of a speech event (Rostomyan, 2012: 281-292).

Turning to the development of our emotional brain, about 100 million years ago the brain in mammals took a great growth spurt. Daniel Goleman (1995) describes that piled on top of the thin two-layered cortex the regions that plan, comprehend what is sensed, coordinate movement – several new layers of the brain cells were added to form the *neocortex* (new cortex). In contrast to the former brain's two-layered cortex, the neocortex offered an extraordinarily improved and refined intellectual edge. In evolution, the neocortex allowed a judicious fine-tuning that undoubtedly has made enormous advantages in an organism's ability to survive adversity, making it more likely that its progeny would turn pass on the genes that contain that same neural circuitry. The survival edge is due to the neocortex's "talent" for strategizing, long-term planning, as well as a lot of other wiles. Beyond that, the triumphs of art, civilization and culture are all fruits of the work of the neocortex. Last but not least, the neocortex allows for the subtlety and complexity of emotional life, such as the ability to have specific feelings *about* our feelings (Goleman, 1995).

Particulary, the **amygdala** arousal seems to imprint in our memory most of the moments of the emotional arousal with an added degree of strength and intensity (Murray, 1964). Maybe this is the very reason why we are more likely to remember, for example, where we went on a first date, or where we were and what we were doing when he heard the striking news

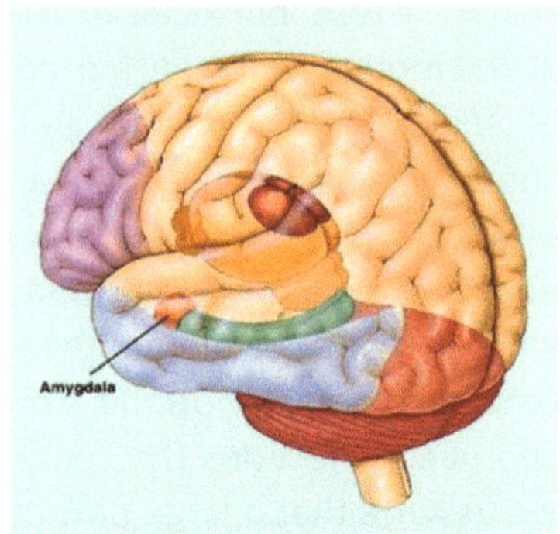

about Princess Diana's mysterious death, etc. Actually, the more intense the amygdala arousal is, the stronger the imprint will be. In fact, the experiences which scare or thrill us the most in life or those which cause extreme positive emotions, are among our most indelible and very long-term memories. This brings to the fact that the brain has two memory systems, i.e. one for ordinary and dry facts, the other – for emotionally charged ones. As it can be followed, the amygdala can be considered to be the inner ruler of our **emotional memory**.

Thus, one of the key claims of the present book is the admission of the fact that emotions work on the cognitive background in the process of verbal interaction. Actually, they include both perception and appraisal functions and are closely related to higher cognitive judgement processes. We firmly believe that the emotional and rational minds are interdependent and closely related since they influence and regulate one another, with emotions stirring up and the rational mind analyzing, refining and sometimes vetoing or endorsing certain emotions (Paronyan, Rostomyan, 2011b).

2.4. The Iceberg Theory

Ernst Hemingway, one of the most influential American writers in the 20th century, pioneered a generation of writing style. Actually, he is famous for this very unique writing style, referred to as *iceberg theory*. This theory is associated with an iceberg (hence the name): one eighth of which is considered to be above the water; all the rest is implied and should be guessed by the reader. One must go very deep beneath the surface to understand the full meaning of the communicative meaning of an utterance.

The so-called "iceberg theory" might be applied to a number of diverse disciplines, to linguistics and communication science as well, to demonstrate that nothing is superficial and that there are lots of other factors, which are not so explicitly obvious just from the first sight; they are actually hidden beneath the surface. Moreover, they have a great impact on all those processes that occur on the surface. Bearing this in mind, now we will attempt to draw a similar iceberg (**Pic. 3**) pointing out to the fact that besides mere explicit word-for-word communication very many various important factors take part in the complex processes of interpersonal communication.

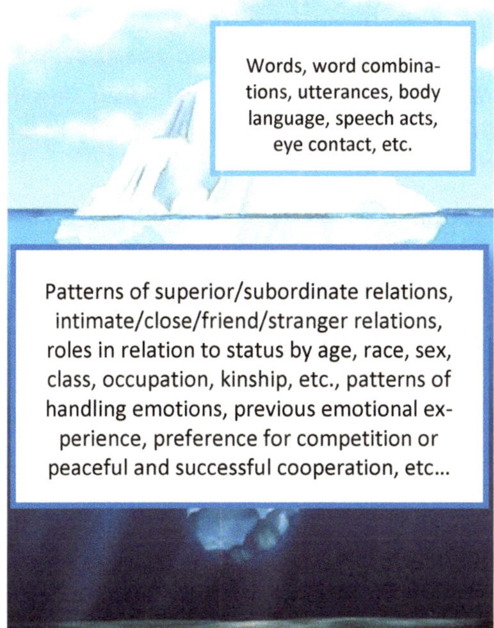

Picture 3: The Correlation of Explicit and Implicit Communication in an Iceberg

As we see, the process of communication involves not only the meaning of the words, which is surely important in the process of communication, but also the role of the interlocutors, who are simultaneously influenced by a number of factors which do have an impact on the interpretation process.

The iceberg can also be applied to when speaking about emotional intelligence, as when speaking about intelligence we do not only speak about pure rational intelligence (IQ), but also about emotional competence and intelligence (EQ), which is not always explicitly demonstrated and is hidden below the surface structure of human behaviour. Yet, it is of utmost importance, since in the process of communication far more occurs on the emotional level and the hidden EQ processes greatly partake in the process of interaction.

Hemingway once said: *"If it is any use to know it, I always try to write on the principle of the iceberg. There are seven-eights of it under water for every part that shows. Anything you know you can eliminate and it only strengthens your iceberg. It is the part that doesn't show. If a writer omits something because he does not know it then there is a hole in the story."* (Hemingway, 1963: 182)

In fact, *succinct words, distinct images, plentiful emotion* and *profound thought* are the four fundamental elements of iceberg theory for further study, that is, the words and images are the so-called "1/8" while the emotion and thought are the so-called "7/8". The formers are specific and visual while the latter are implied in the former. The words portray the images; the emotion is embodied in the images; the thought is embodied in the emotion expressed verbally or non-verbally (Paronyan, Rostomyan, 2011b: 13).

The same is true when speaking about spoken language: the words portray the images; our emotions are embodied in the images; our inner thoughts are embodied in those emotions. Hence, it becomes obvious that the role of our mental world has, indeed, a great and let us say even irreplaceable role in the decoding process, particularly when dealing with expressive speech acts.

Admittedly, a great deal of research work devoted to the analysis of the mental apparatus of linguistic behaviour has been carried out in Cognitive Linguistics so far (Sanders 2005; Heritage 2005; Kasevich 1989; Paronyan 2011). As a result, speech came to be regarded as a rule-governed process of social behaviour which is based on certain knowledge structures stored in the rational mind. Hence, cognition should be treated as inner mental knowledge which appears on the surface level of the rational mind through verbal behaviour. Similarly, mental knowledge is verbalized when it reaches the highest, that is, the surface level of the rational mind. While the importance of the conscious and subconscious control of the rational mind in the process of production and interpretation of linguistic signs has become unquestionable, the involvement of the emotional mind in communicative matters still remains open.

2.5. The Emotional/Rational Dichotomy

In 1994, A. Damasio published his famous book "Descartes' Error: Emotion, Reason and the Human Brain". His book is now considered to be a significant milestone in the research on human emotions as it brings an important experimental perspective of the former ideas of William James (1890) and Daniel Dennet (1989, 1991). His work provides a biological framework to explain emotions not as a psychological state of the soul, but as a physical phenomenon. Unfortunately, due to the complexity of the concepts involved, this point of view is not sufficient to guarantee an immediate feasible implementation, but on the other hand, it brings a number of new insights on how it can be implemented in further research. To understand Damasio's view of emotion, we first need to understand several other basic concepts: mind and body, imaginative thinking, somatic marker and intuition.

For Damasio, our mind is physically associated with our body through our brain. For him, the idea that the mind and the body can be dissociated and each one can be represented by a different state machine is wrong and misleading. He strongly believes that it is not possible to consider each one as an independent entity without any loss of information. As a result, he claims that our body is not only a machine that holds an intelligent mind: our thinking is fully connected with our body. In other words, our mind is fully embodied into our body, and not simply held by it.

Referring to Daniel Dennet's work, Damasio points out that the usual metaphor for our thinking is a movie where each frame has not only visual images, but also images of the others 4 senses: olfaction, hearing, taste and touch. He shows that the big screen where this movie is projected does not physically exist into our brain. Instead, we process each kind of sense in physically different and distributed locations in our brain. The perception we have of the centralized nature of thinking is, as a matter of fact, an emergence phenomenon resulting from the time of synchronization of all the distributed processors. For Damasio, there are two basic and important kinds of mental images: ***perceptual*** and ***dispositive***. A perceptual image is, in the biological level, a topographically organized neural activity into any sensorial cortex of the brain. A perceptual image might be generated by our sensors or by the other kind of image, namely, the dispositive image. A dispositive image is what Damasio calls "dispositional representation." In the light of this, a dispositive image is a prototypical image that holds the rules to reconstruct perceptual images. The collection of all dispositive images constitutes our full repository of knowledge. A dispositive image, when properly excited or triggered, might produce or recall perceptual images, or excite other dispositive images. It is important to note that one dispositive image does not centralize the knowledge related to an object. Each dispositive image holds a different aspect of the same object and when we think about this object; all images are triggered synchronously, creating the perception of a centralized unit that holds any other related information about that very object (Damasio, 1994).

As a result, according to Damasio's work, an emotion can be seen as a dispositive image that affects the body's internal state. However, an emotion is not the perception of the body's internal state or its change. Instead, this perception is the *feeling*, and not merely the emotion itself. Many authors consider feelings and emotions as synonyms. In his work, these two concepts are considered to be different, but correlated.

Besides, according to Damasio (1994), there are two basic categories of emotions: **primary** and **secondary**. Primary emotions are innate and are often related to self-preserving and reproduction. Their triggering occurs on an unconscious level, when perceptive images excite them, causing a reaction that affects the body state. Secondary emotions are similar to primary ones. Both of them affect the body state when excited. The difference between them is the fact that secondary emotions are not innate. Additionally, secondary emotions may work both on a conscious and unconscious level. According to Damasio, this phenomenon happens because of the fact that they are evolved from the primary emotions and, consequently, use the mechanisms of the former. This conscious part of secondary emotions occurs when they are triggered by some stimulus generated by a rational and conscious thinking. Thus, emotion believed to be able to change the body's internal state and, consequently, affects how the brain processes others mental images. This interaction happens in two different ways:

- *changing the performance of the cognitive mechanism* and
- *attributing an intuition (used in the mental processing) to another mental images through a mechanism called the somatic marker.*

Consequently, we may assert that our perception of the world and our surroundings, our relationship with the others, our formerly experienced emotions can be viewed as images which are stored in our brain. The latter may later on process this information which may, as a result, have an impact and even regulate our further behaviour and actions.

Philosophy of Mind and Cognitive Science, on one hand, generally view the nature of cognition by discussing its various faculties, such as *language* and *perception*; however, another important question to be raised is also the nature of the cognitive role immanent in emotions. Particularly, it should be mentioned that it still remains unclear whether the fundamental notions of the mind frequently discussed, such as: *representation* and *embodiment*, can also be employed to explain the cognitive role immanent in emotions, or such notions should somehow be altered in order to fit the nature of emotions. According to the cognitive theory of emotions, there is almost always a *judgment* immanent in emotions, which is sometimes propositional, but may well be non-propositional, non-articulated, unconscious, and can even be kinesthetic, as evident in animal judgments; furthermore, emotions are seen as bearing the essence of active engagement in the world (Solomon, 2004).

The **cognitivism of emotions**, so far, describes what emotions are like without explaining why the emotional judgment takes so diverse forms and how it is possible to simultaneously hold affects and judgment in a single emotional sense. Despite of its name, this cognitivism of emotions, while insisting that emotions consist in judgment, does not constrain what emotional judgment consists of. This opens up a possibility of taking embodiment into the cognitivism of emotions. This would look contradictory for the cognitivism in the general understanding of cognition, but surprisingly not for the cognitivism of emotions. The present book seeks for ways to answer the aforementioned questions, by raising a viewpoint that emotions are not mere sensations and comprise cognitive elements as well. Moreover, sometimes our emotions can even be guided by our rational mind due to the stored background memory of our relationship with the other's and some formerly experienced emotions, since we are all the time making judgments on situations, events and individuals (Paronyan, Rostomyan, 2011b).

It is generally believed that the emotional sense is constantly active because it evaluates whether the confronted situation is favourable or unfavourable for his/her survival and how the own self's well-being would change when being confronts those very surroundings. It is also active because the emotional subject keeps changing the background/context of her emotional judgment, and because he/she is an agent who is keen to enhance her well-being. As a matter of fact, emotions and cognition go hand-in-hand. In general, the subject is inclined to process and evaluate the emotions he or she is undergoing and may change some of the learned emotions as well, but sometimes those emotions may be so pertinent (as are various phobias) that the subject will not stand a chance to change the beating of his/her heart when seeing, say, a mouse or a rat. Yet, it has been noted that people may change their relationship in due course of time. For instance, they may have tense relationship and every time seeing each other may feel such negative emotions as anger, annoyance, or irritation, but in case one of them does something good that will be processed, analyzed and kept in the mind of the other, the latter will consequently change his/her attitude. As a result, the emotions being evoked also change (Rostomyan, 2013b).

The emotional judgment generally refers to the *complex background understandings* of our well-being and comfort. The emotional subjects constantly interact with their *complex environment,* having to be faced with diverse situations and various people having different cultural, national, educational, and even emotional backgrounds. Such complexities and the above-mentioned affects as epiphenomena, identify the reason why emotions should by no means be regarded as separate phenomena from cognitive processes. Moreover, we are highly inclined to think that viewing the problem from this angle and taking into account the essence of the cognitive processes, will ensure revealing the nature of emotions much better. All this suggests that emotions are not devoid of any cognitive elements. Instead, these two phenomena are tightly interconnected (Rostomyan, 2013b).

Indeed, recently it has really been much debate on to what extent emotions are rational or whether they are rational or not. Actually, the emotional/rational dichotomy approximates the folk distinction between the human *"heart"* and *"head"*. Sometimes people are sure that something is wrong "in their heads", but "their hearts" tell them just the opposite, or just vice versa: you know something is the right thing to do "in your heart", but "your head" tells you not to. There is a steady gradient in the ration of rational-to-emotional control over the mind; the more intense the feeling, the more dominant the emotional mind becomes – and the more ineffectual the rational (Goleman, 1995: 9). Indeed, in those very moments your heart may tell you one thing, whereas your brain – quite another thing: you can, hence, write down the opposite pole thoughts to be able to understand your emotions and give an emotionally rational answer to the situation (Bradberry & Greaves, 2016: 86).

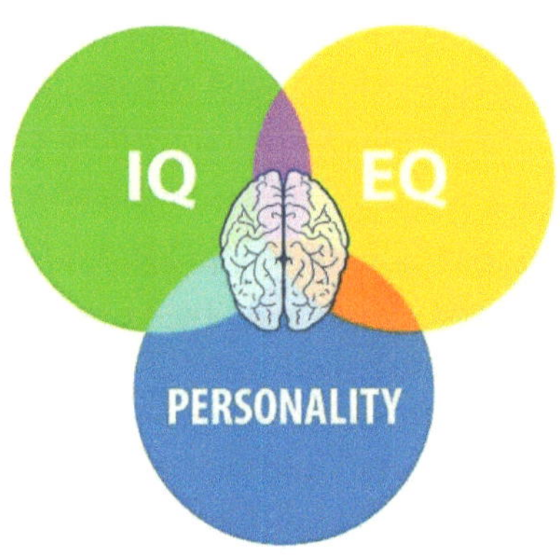

Chart 2: The EQ & IQ Dichotomy[2]

In essence, these two minds, the emotional (EQ) and the rational (IQ), generally operate in firm harmony, intertwining their very different ways of knowing to guide us through the world. Ordinarily, there is a balance between the emotional and rational minds, with emotion feeding into and informing the operations of the rational mind, and the rational mind refining and sometimes vetoing the inputs of the emotions. Yet, these two minds, the emotional and the rational one, are semi-dependent faculties, each reflecting the operation of distinct,

---

[2] Chart graphic design by Sona Safaryan, MA in Arts.

but interconnected circuitry in the brain, which together have an influence on our personality (Paronyan, Rostomyan, 2011b; Rostomyan, 2012, Rostomyan, 2018).

In tune with modern theorists of emotions (cf. Ortony, Clore, Collins, LeDoux, et alias), we regard emotions essentially as subconscious signals and evaluations that inform, modify and receive feedback from higher cognitive processes. In a sense, we have to admit that human beings have two minds which are closely interrelated – *emotional* and *rational*. We should also admit that cognitive intelligence cannot work at its best potential without emotional intelligence.

This reasoning enables us to put aside the old opposition between *raison d'être* and *feeling* (i.e. *reason vs. emotion*) and try to find a sensible balance between the two minds.

Admittedly, the paradigm, where reason is seen completely unchained from emotions, does not hold true, and a new one should be adopted, in which head and heart, feeling and thought, emotion and ration are in harmony. Therefore, we do believe that emotions should not be viewed as mere sensations totally devoid of rational element.

Moreover, we suppose that these two constantly interact and continuously cooperate with one another; thus, together bringing information to the higher cognitive processes, adhering to Kant's theory on emotional reasoning, who resolved the debate of sensualists and rationalists, claiming that both emotion and reason are important for the righteous interpretation of this or that piece of information (Rostomyan, 2013b).

It is true that in the heated emotional moment rationality does not perform at its best, but only adhering to pure dry facts may leave out a great of important information, which can also bring facts to the overall interpretation of the received data. Therefore, we do firmly believe that the harmonious interaction of the two, can drastically help us in handling life situations and correspondingly respond to them.

The interrelation between emotion and cognition can be seen in **Chart 2** presented below:

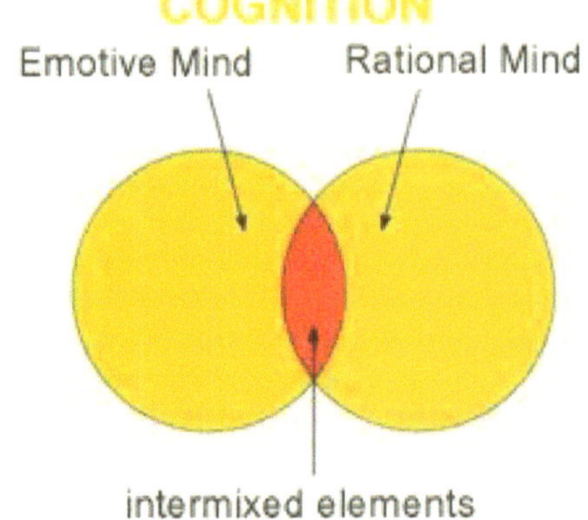

Chart 3: The Interrelation of Emotional and Rational Minds altogether shaping human Cognition[3]

(Chart source: Rostomyan, 2015: 1275)

According to Daniel Goleman if the emotional mind follows the logic and its rules, with one element standing for another and cooperating with one another, things need not necessarily be defined by their objective identity; what matters is how they are perceived; things are as they seems. What something reminds us of can be far more important that what it "is" (Goleman, 1995: 338).

Hence, the balanced collaboration of the aforementioned two *"human minds"* is very essential in interpersonal communication in every sphere of activity: actually these two minds continuously cooperating with each other endorsing or vetoing certain emotions and their communicative expressions (Paronyan, Rostomyan, 2011a: 26-33).

---

[3] Chart graphic design by Arman Sargsyan, BA in Arts and Design.

In many or most cases these minds are exquisitely coordinated; feelings are essential to thought, thought to feeling. Nevertheless, strikingly when passions surge the balance tilts: it is then the emotional mind that captures the upper hand, swapping the rational mind. It is noteworthy that the sixteenth-century humanist Erasmus of Rotterdam wrote in a satirical vein of this perennial tension between **reason** and **emotion**:

"Jupiter has bestowed far more passion than reason – you could calculate the ration as 24 to one. He set up two raging tyrants in opposition to Reason's solitary power: anger and lust. How far Reason can prevail against the combined forces of these two, common life of man makes quite clear. Reason does the only thing she can and shouts herself hoarse, repeating formulas of virtue, while the other two bid her go hang herself, and are increasingly noisy and offensive, until at last their Ruler is exhausted, gives up, and surrenders."

(Goleman, 1995: 9)

In the aforementioned extract, the author well-describes the constant combat of emotion and ration, with emotions stirring up and the rational mind voting, filtering or endorsing them.

Nowadays very often scientists speak about Emotional Intelligence (EQ) as compared with purely Rational Intelligence (IQ), and which is more striking, preference is given to the former one as this mainly contributes to the creation of peaceful relations.

D. Goleman identified the five *"domains"* of EQ as:

1. **Knowing** your emotions.
2. **Managing** your own emotions.
3. **Motivating** yourself.
4. **Recognizing** and understanding other people's emotions.
5. **Managing** relationships, i.e., managing the emotions of others (Goleman, 1995).

Yet, it is also noteworthy that under certain circumstances the balance between cognitive and emotive minds gets lost: emotions come to prevail and, as a result, one loses the ability to properly estimate the situation at hand. Truly, in the heat of emotional obsession the ability to regulate his/her thoughts, behaviour and speech can be extremely diminished, and in these situations, one should take pains not to let emotions govern the cognitive part of the brain: once we lose the balance, we are sure to make wrong decisions and wrongly evaluate diverse situations. Consequently, we may even misinterpret different messages from the external world and respond to them inappropriately. This is the reason why when we are emotionally upset or anxious about something, we often state that we *just can't think straight*. The fact of being emotionally distressed can even hinder one's ability to learn and work properly and effectively. Sometimes, the influence of the emotions (positive or negative) is so enormous that the emotional mind becomes prevailing and one does not manage to control it. This fact actually finds its verbal and/or non-verbal manifestation – we say things for which we may later regret. Consequently, it is advisable that the emotional-rational balance should be kept in order not to be exposed to bewildering and misleading situations and subsequent misinterpretations. A good and sensible piece of advice which, unfortunately, is often so difficult for many of us to follow! (Rostomyan, 2013b)

As we have already given stated, the role of emotions and their psychological emotional impact play a vital role in interpersonal relations, yet it should be born in mind that the role and significance of rationality can by no means be diminished as it brings the most important information. Besides, the **context** is another "player" too.

The interrelation of emotion, rationality and the context at hand can be well depicted in this way as shown in **Chart 3** below, where just in the middle lies the reality in the core. It should by all means be mentioned that emotions can also be interpreted largely depending on the context, the situation at hand and the rational interpretation of the state of affairs, as these greatly influence interpretative powers and bring their information to the process of interpreting the received outer data and stimuli.

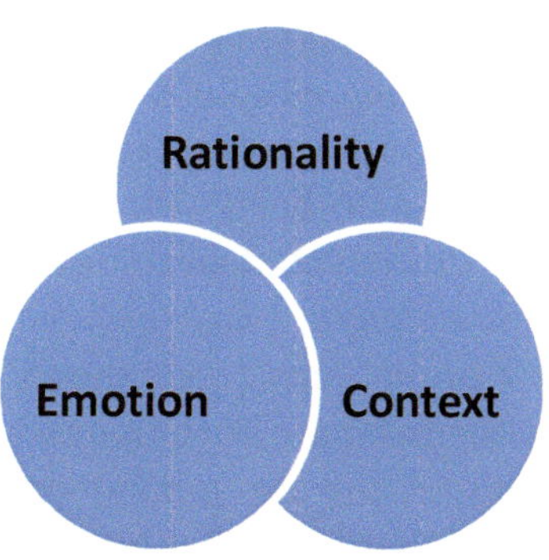

Chart 4: The Interrelation of 1. Rationality, 2. Emotion, and 3. Context: Reality is in the Core

Obviously, the positive/negative emotional attitude of the speaker towards the parameters of the linguistic situation is related to his/her evaluative competence and, therefore, has cognitive significance. Thus, we assume that the analysis of the linguistic mechanisms of verbalization of emotions, which has become quite actual today, should be carried out on the basis of cognitive evaluation of emotivity (Rostomyan, 2013b, 2014).

In this connection, it should be stated that emotivity is often related to the affective behaviour of the speakers. Emotions are defined as *strong feelings which constitute the part of the person's character* (Oxford Advanced Learner's Dictionary 1997). Naturally, if we want to bring to light the innate nature of the emotive mind, we should penetrate into the inner mental world of the speaker and examine how this or that emotion is articulated in speech. No doubt the linguistic analysis of emotiveness cannot be carried out without any resort to cognitive science – Cognitive Psychology, Cognitive Linguistics.

The analysis of emotions from the psychological perspective raises the question of the relationship between emotive experience and bodily expression, that is, perception and expression of emotions. In this connection two contradictory points of view can be stated. According to the traditional theory, emotions are feelings or at least experiences of a special type which involve feelings. Hence, when faced with an external stimulus, human beings first of all experience emotions, their reaction to the external situation comes next, that is, and response follows emotion. For example, I see the bear, I feel *frightened* (Rostomyan, 2013b). The proponents of this theory make it clear that emotions should be regarded as mere sensations which are evoked from any perceived external stimuli and are completely devoid of any rational elements (Murray 1964). Whereas other psychologists hold the opposite viewpoint, firmly claiming that emotions do comprise rational elements (Damasio, 1994; Goleman, 1995).

The indexicals of the psychological state of the interlocutors predetermine the emotive charge of speech (both explicit and implicit) – convey emotional effect to speech, make an emotional and logical effect on the listener and, at the same time, form basis for the hearer himself to interpret the speech act emotionally. Hence, *emotional memory* works both for the speaker who encodes certain emotive meaning into his/her speech and the interpreter who decodes the speaker's intended meaning emotively. Thus, we assume that a large part of implicit meaning, which remains unsaid and veiled in the process of interaction, is related to human emotions and feelings. The speakers' past negative or positive emotional experience, which, as we said, is also part of mutually shared background knowledge, determines their choice of language data on a particular occasion of a speech event (Paronyan, Rostomyan, 2011b).

Hence, being components of the interlocutors' mental world, feelings and emotions very often find their outward verbal or non-verbal manifestation in speech, especially when the speakers while undergoing very strong emotions speakers do not manage to suppress them or when they want to have an emotive impact on the interlocutors. Consequently, it becomes obvious that by means of performing emotionally coloured speech, one stands a better chance of reaching his/her desired positive or negative emotional impact on the listeners (Rostomyan, 2012, 2013a,b).

As a matter of fact, much has been said so far about diverse aspects of implicit meaning in Pragmatics by many outstanding linguists, such as Searle (1969, 1975), Grice (1969, 1975), Levinson (1983), Verschueren (1999), van Dijk (1977) and many others. Research carried out in this field of analysis comes to prove that speakers usually exercise their interpretative power to decode the illocutionary force of the speech act, to deduce the emotional implicature embodied in the message, to recognize the clichéd behavioural frames and practice the scenarios stored in the long-term memory in order to decode the strategic involvement of the speaking partners in the given speech event, and so on. Yet, the role of emotional background memory, which, undoubtedly, influences the coding and decoding process on the part of interlocutors and, thus, gains paramount importance here still requires further investigation and study (Paronyan, Rostomyan, 2011b).

The analyses of verbal behaviour in diverse spheres and under various circumstances which proceeds in the form of negative emotional colouring and results in conflict talk illustrate the major role of the emotional mind (the speakers' positive or negative emotions, beliefs, desires and wishes, motivations and intentions) in shaping of the given communicative context (see Grice 1975).

Our analysis comes to prove that the prior positive or negative disposition of the interlocutors may change in the process of interaction depending on diverse extralinguistic factors. For instance, the tense relations experienced by two people every time they meet each other – such negative emotions as anger, annoyance, discomfort, contempt or irritation, may change in the positive direction, or just vice versa, previous positive emotional disposition may become negative (Paronyan, Rostomyan, 2011a,b).

Let us analyze an example illustrating a spontaneous change of emotional mind in the process of interaction:

"I wanted to do this personally, Scott, so I could explain."
"She filed for divorce?"
Harry nodded. "Trey, the pro, he hired me – or he's paying me. He's already won a   tournament, a million bucks, so he can afford me."
Scott almost laughed. *"We played golf how many times, Harry?* ***A hundred****? And you're taking the money from the guy my wife ran off with?" (Gimenez 2007:458)*

In this example the speakers have been good friends for quite a long time and experience positive emotions towards each other. Yet Harry, who is a lawyer, has accepted to undertake the divorce case of his friend's wife for money. When Scott learns about this, he feels depressed because he regards this act as treachery. So, his feelings towards his close friend change and Scott, undoubtedly, begins to experience rather negative emotions such as disappointment, annoyance, anger. Thus, the cognitive evaluation in the actual speech situation is negative: Scott has been betrayed by one of his best friends. The description of the author also implies this: *Scott almost laughed*. As we know emotions can be expressed both verbally and non-verbally. In this case the act of *laughing* does not denote the experience of such positive emotions as happiness, joy, delight; instead, it denotes the existence of negative emotions such as sadness, despair, disappointment. The approximator *almost* also shows that it was only a sarcastic laugh the illocutionary force of which was to condemn Harry. Thus, Scott scolds his friend indirectly, by issuing an act of reproach in the form of a question: *We played golf how many times, Harry? A hundred? And you're taking the money from the guy my wife ran off with?* The speaker's negative emotions are also manifested in his word choice: he achieves intensification of the negative effect by appealing to his interlocutor personally (*Harry*), as well as by using the numeral *hundred* in an elliptical utterance: the speaker experiences a change of emotional mind due to negative evaluation of certain parameters of the communicative situation. This change is expressed in his word choice and results in conflict talk.

As far as emotional speech performance is concerned, it should be noted that a great deal of research has been done in linguistics to define the elements of speech which perform an evaluative impact, i.e. *words, word-combinations, syntactic constructions, speech acts*, which are bearers of certain emotional attitude, either positive or negative. In fact, the problem of emotion involves a number of important issues: *perception, processing* and *evaluation* of emotions and emotional states; *verbal and non-verbal means of expressing emotion*. Facial expressions, together with bodily movements form non-verbal means of communicating the emotional state of the speaker. As for the verbalization of emotions, there exist certain function words called *intensifiers* which are used to modify or intensify the whole sentence or only part of it, particularly its emotional content (Rostomyan, 2009: 91-100). The analysis of the factual material enabled us to claim that if we want to deal with the problem of the manifestation of emotion in speech, we have to focus on expressive speech acts from the perspective of pragmalinguistic analysis, since those kinds of speech acts state what the speaker feels (Rostomyan, 2013b).

2.6. Manifestation of Emotions in Business

As already mentioned in the beginning of this book, emotions are grouped into two main groups according to evaluation – *positive emotions* (such as love, affection, gladness, joy, delight, happiness, etc.) and *negative emotions* (such as hatred, annoyance, fury, anger, rage, etc.). Therefore, verbal, visual and/or non-verbal expressions of emotions can also entail both two types of emotion, positive and/or negative, depending on the context of communication (Rostomyan, 2009).

Whenever the speakers are overwhelmed with very strong either positive or negative emotions, their emotional attitude is being reflected in their speech. However, as already mentioned, sometimes speakers have to manage the display of their emotions depending on various factors (social status, social distance, etc.). Many jobs require what Hochschild calls an *"emotional labour"*. His exploitation of this concept involves flight attendants who, because of the demands of their occupation, engage in "surface" and "deep" acting in order to shape the outward appearance of a calm, unworried, pleasant emotional state (see Hochschild 1985).

This may include instances when the manager is so disappointed about and angry with their employee's work that they by no means tend to control the display of their felt emotions and actually express them in their speech via verbal and non-verbal means of manifesting emotions which, as a result, having an emotive impact on the listener. The passage below represents a stretch of discourse where Les, the employer, is furious at Rachel, his employee, who works as a senior lawyer at his firm and who has performed malpractice by not reading properly the procedure of the Court concerning the appropriate delivery of papers and has sent them via mail which may consequently cause actual harm to their company. The conversation is being made on the phone; the employer is so angry that he does not even perform the usual greeting and conversation opening formulae.

> *'How did you serve the IXP papers?' he barks into the phone as soon as I say hello. Les always skips the pleasantries.*
>
> *'What do you mean?'*
>
> *'Your mode of service. By mail? By hand?'*
>
> *I nailed it to the cottage door, jackass, I think, remembering the antiquated mode of service tested by the New York bar.*
>
> *'By mail,' I say, glancing down at my well-worn copy of the New York Rules of Civil Prudence.*
>
> ***'Great. F***ing great,'** he says in his normal snide tone.*
>
> *'What?'*
>
> *'What? What?' he **shouts into the phone. I pull the receiver away from my ear** but now I hear his voice in stereo, filling the hall. **'You f***ed up!** That's what! The papers needed to go by hand! Didn't you bother to read the Court's order?'*
>
> *I scan the letter from the judge. Damn, he is right.*

'You're right,' I say solemnly. He hates excuses and I have
none anyway. 'I screwed up.'
*'What are you, a **goddamn** first-year associate?'*
I stare at my desk. He knows full well that I'm a fifth-year.
(Giffin, Something Borrowed, 2011: 170-171)

The negative emotions of the employer are manifested on the vocal level as well; he shouts into the phone so loudly that Rachel even pulls the receiver away from her ear. He uses a number of vulgar intensifying expressions in his speech, i.e. f***ing, f***ed, goddamn, etc. As we know, these types of intensifiers are usually used in familiar conversation between equals, whereas here the speaker, who uses them in his speech, is higher in status and, thus, should try to avoid such expressions while making an act of reproach. Still, the mistake is so gross that Rachel herself confesses that she was to blame and she has actually performed a real malpractice. Of course, it is an undeniable fact that each and every employee, who does not act for the benefit of the firm has to be called for response, since it is through understanding our own faults that we can become more successful and proficient professionals and work in a peaceful atmosphere. Nonetheless, we do believe that such instances should be solved in a more diplomatic way. For instance, the same conversation should be made not on the phone but while face-to-face conversation, or the same things could be said by the employer again in a strict tone, but without using so many offensive expressions. This would, indeed, fit into the seriousness of the situation; as a result, giving both of them a better chance to proceed and learn to avoid a similar situation in the future as there has been made a real gross mistake and in case of visualizing each other while conversing would give the employer a better chance of reaching his desired impact on the employee making the latter realize the significance of their conversation and make her understand that this kind of mistake should by all means be avoided in the future since not following his instructions may cost Rachel her job. It is our firm belief that the same impact cannot be reached in case of phone conversation since in case of face-to-face communication the speaker who wants to make an act of reproach, besides using verbal means of conveying information and emotions, may also apply non-verbal means, i.e. facial expressions, eye contact, gestures, bodily movements, etc. (Ternès, Rostomyan, 2011a,b, 2012).

The fact is that after this conversation the tense emotions that they both have felt during the conversation will be shaped in their emotional background memory and will later on hinder the process of their mutual understanding, since they have already been negatively disposed towards each other. In case the manager or the employee is such a skilled person who is able to control the display of those very negative emotions and manifest them in a polite manner, he or she will actually stand a better chance of both reaching his/her desired result and preserving the harmonious relations with the personnel who are, as a matter of fact, one of the most important part of each and every organization, company, or institution. One should think twice before using any words as those very words, if not appropriately used, may have negative impact on the people who will consequently begin to feel certain negative emotions which may consequently harm the harmonious working atmosphere (Rostomyan, 2015; Rostomyan & Rostomyan, 2018).

The extract below represents an illustration of imparting positive emotions on the part of the employer. Here, as he is not influenced by certain external stimuli causing negative emotions, he gives instructions to his employee in a more accurate manner, even making a compliment concerning the roses on the latters table.

> *I swivel in my chair and give him the update. 'I've checked all the cases in New York. And federal cases too.'*
> *'Okay. But keep in mind that our fact pattern is unique,' Les says. 'I'm not sure the Court will care much about precedent.'*
> *'I know that. But as far as I can tell the general holding we rely upon in Section One is still good law. So that's a good first step.'*
> *So there.*

'Well, make sure you check case law in other jurisdictions too,' he says. 'We need to anticipate all of their arguments.'
'Yup,' I say.
No, duh.
*As he turns to leave, he says over his shoulder, **'Nice roses.'** I am stunned. Les and I do not make small talk, and he has never commented on anything other than my work, not even a 'how was your weekend?' on a Monday morning, or a 'cold enough out there for you?' when we ride the elevator together on a snowy day. (Giffin, Something Borrowed, 2011: 177-178)*

In the above-mentioned passage, Les, the employer, does not very strictly give commands to his employee, namely Rachel, explaining the work to be done in an accurate way, and he even performs an act of complimenting the employee by noticing the flowers on the table, i.e. *Nice roses*, this representative speech act bearing positive emotive charge, as a matter of fact, may serve as a stimulus for Rachel to think that her boss is not a monster after all and may praise her work in case she manages to succeed in doing everything according to the predefined procedure of the Court. As the author explains, Rachel is stunned and positively amazed by this very fact because they have never exchanged a couple of words not concerning work. Thus, as Les has never done something like this before, now, as a matter of fact, it attracts Rachel's attention more, even if it is only a very short comment bearing positive overtones and is done without looking at her, in a shy way or like in a rush (Rostomyan & Rostomyan, 2018).

This truly reminds us of Henry Ford, one of the greatest managers that human history has known, who always tried to be in close contact with his employees remembering their family issues even if it's only a very small beginning along the way of reaching a healthy and productive working atmosphere. We do believe that acting in this way in regard to your employees can also be considered to be one of the pledges of one's flourishing business (Rostomyan, 2015).

Another interesting example is Napoleon Bonaparte, who remembered all his soldiers by name and surname giving them the ground to be sure that their leader cares for each and every one of them. Thus, we come to think that in case managers praise their employees whenever deserved or sometimes communicate with them concerning different topics, they will consequently change their interpersonal relations and the overall performance for the better.

Hence, any influence of incidental emotions would suggest that decisions are influenced by factors unrelated to the utility of their consequences. Yet, far too much of what happens in the process of communications occurs on the emotional level (Rostomyan, 2009). According to Hochschild there exist certain professions, economics included, in which the main actors at hand have to manage their emotions to sound proficient (Hochschild, 1983).

As a matter of fact, by means of appropriately managing the verbal and non-verbal displays of positive or negative emotions the speaking partners stand a better chance of having an emotive influence on the audience and hence obtaining their target. All this comes to prove that emotions do play a very vital role in decision making processes (Rostomyan, 2013a,b, 2015).

We have analyzed a number of cases and revealed that very often financial means do not necessarily bring happiness with them nor do they contribute to the development of individual spiritual calmness and mindfulness.

In the book of Tony Hsieh "Delivering Happiness", the author speaks about the main important factors which altogether shape a successful business within economic relations. He vividly Draws his assertions to the fact that in case your economic steps do not contain *passion, energy* and *emotion*, your business will most probably not prosper nor will you be satisfied with the results.

The author speaks also about his commercial ups and downs and points out to the fact that spiritual calmness can be achieved by balancing our emotions, both on the psychological and speech levels, and developing a kind of culture inside of the financial and economical interrelations between the partners and colleagues. He very minutely describes the development of his business projects and economic decisions, revealing that there should be a kind of emotional co-relation inside the company to help blossom the overall project and satisfy everybody's individual needs, by this means also contributing of the establishment of happiness in the mental world of the interactants which surely does cause better labour output (Rostomyan, 2015).

According to him one of his business projects which was a web platform, called LinkExchange, which was designed to help students share knowledge collapsed in due course of time as they were hiring a number of employees without paying much attention to their individual preferences and without building a kind of friendly working atmosphere between them:

"At that time, I didn't think it was necessarily a bad thing. If anything, not recognizing people due to our hyper growth made things even more interesting and fueled the 24/7 adrenaline high that we were all *feeling*. But looking back, it should have been a huge warning sign for what was to come.

The short story is that we simply didn't know we should have paid more attention to our *company culture*. During the first year, we'd hired our friends and people who wanted to be part of building something fun and exciting. Without realizing it, we had together created a company culture that we all enjoyed being part of." (Hsieh, 2010: 47)

As we see, the author puts emphasis on *feelings* and *emotions* as human resources are not working machines devoid of their own inner world which may involve a very many various positive and/or negative emotions which do have a high influence on the working skills of both the employees and the employer (Rostomyan, 2015: 1268-1277).

Thereafter, describing all the minute details of his personal career, he depicts the picture of himself when being at top of his built empire he realized that he was not happy with his economic decisions connected with selling LinkExchange, which was truly his own *child* in a way, to Microsoft and gaining a huge fortune as a cause, he decides to build another empire so that not to lose that sparkle within himself and be the beginning of something new even by means of losing the 40 percent of his wealth. As he himself states he was not fully aware of the essence of his acts at that time:

"I didn't realize it at the time, but it was a turning point for me in my life. I had decided to stop chasing the *money*, and start chasing the *passion*." (Hsieh, 2010: 54)

Thus, together with a couple of his friends, they decided to create an online shoe shopping platform called Zappos (the word was derived from the Spanish word for shoes "zapatos" and they added another "p" to ensure the right pronunciation). Later on, when hiring people and deciding with whom to co-operate, the author again put much emphasis on whom to hire: a very significant point for him was to see vital strong emotions, motivation and passion in their eyes which will surely bring much motion, success, and prosperity to their company:

"...I like the guys there. They're *passionate* and determined, and they don't seem like they're doing this just to get rich quick. They're actually interested in trying to build something for the long run." (Hsieh, 2010: 73)

In this context, the author points out another important factor, that is *connectedness*. When speaking about the connectedness of the employees involved in a certain project and denoting the reson for this or that decision making reasons, the author uses a very unique abbreviation of his own, namely "*PLUR*", which stand for "*Peace, Love, Unity, Respect*" (Hsieh, 2010). All the aforementioned are highly connected with higher cognitive processes as well as emotional responses of the body to external stimuli (Murray, 1964; Goleman, 1995).

"The idea of *PLUR* and the rave *culture* rubbed off on me beyond the rave scene. To me, it was really more a philosophy about always being open to meeting people no matter how they looked or what their backgrounds were. Every interaction with anyone anywhere was an opportunity to gain additional perspective. We are all human at the core, and it can be easy to lose sight of that in a world ruled by business, politics, and social status. The rave culture was a reminder that it was possible for the world to be a better place, for people to simply be appreciative of the humanity in one another." (Hsieh, 2010: 81)

According to the economic models of decision-making decision makers choose between alternative courses of action by assessing the desirability and likelihood of their consequences, and integrating this information through some type of expectation-based calculus (Rick and Loewenstein 2008). The role of the *mutually shared positive or negative emotional background knowledge* and *emotional memory* of the speaking partners here comes to the forefront and plays a very vital part in each and every act of decision making. Moreover, when making decisions the economists rely on their former emotional experiences and even while debating or expressing their viewpoint, they take actions in order to modify the *verbal or non-verbal expressions of their emotions* to have a better *emotional impact* on their interlocutors to reach their desired goal. This is the basis of Neuroeconomics, where emotions actively partake in the decision-making processes (Rostomyan, 2015).

As for **facial expressions**, academic research shows that people categorize emotion faces in a similar way across cultures, that similar facial expressions tend to occur in response to particular emotion eliciting events or occasions, and that people produce simulations of emotion faces that are characteristic of each specific emotion in particular (Ekman, 2004). Although there may be slight cultural differences, the general patterns of expressing emotions and simulating them on our faces are rather the same. Despite some unsettled theoretical discussions and implications of these findings, a consensus view is that in diverse studies of human emotions and the actual verbal and non-verbal means of communicating the latters, it is often useful and important to know what exact facial expressions correspond to each specific emotion and to know the basic cultural differences so that not to leave some ground for misunderstandings. For instance, it is very important to know that although almost in all the European and Asian one generally nods to confirm a statement and shakes the head to deny a statement, in the Bulgarian culture it is quite the opposite: one shakes the head to imply the answer "Yes" and nods to imply the answer "No". Thus, in case the speakers are not aware of the cultural differences this may cause actual misunderstanding (Rostomyan, 2013b).

Daniel Goleman (1995) claims that the argument for there being a handful of core emotions hinges to some extent on the discovery by Paul Ekman at the University of California at San Francisco that specific facial expressions for four of them (fear, anger, sadness, enjoyment) are recognized by people in cultures around the world, including preliterate people presumably untainted by exposure to cinema or television – suggesting their universality. Ekman proved that facial photos portraying expressions with technical precision to people in cultures as remote as the Fore of New Guinea, an isolated Stone Age tribe in the remote highlands, and found out that people everywhere recognized the same basic emotions. This universality of the basic facial expressions of emotions was probably first noted by Darwin, who saw it as evidence the forces of evolution had stamped these signals in our central nervous system (Ekman 2004; Goleman 1995: 290).

In the example presented below we can observe a case of encoding negative emotions via non-verbal means of communication and in this way performing an indirect act of reproach: *caught Scott's eye*. In everyday life, as a matter of fact, sometimes even merely an eye contact may be sufficient to decode the intended positive or negative emotion.

> ***Dan Ford caught Scott's eye****; his ex-senior partner's expression asked a silent question: You gave up your career for a murderer? (Gimenez, The Colour of Law, 2007: 411)*

In the aforementioned passage Dan Ford, the former partner of Scott, who is a lawyer and who, notwithstanding a number of obstacles which ruin his career, has decided to defend an Afro-American woman who most probably is a murderer. Dan's eye contact with Scott bears the implicit meaning of an indirect act of reproach, naturally evoking negative emotive impact on him. Of course, as far as eye contact is concerned the problem should be viewed from an intercultural or multicultural perspective as well. For instance, in contrast to facial expressions and mimics, an eye contact bears a different meaning in different cultures; e.g. a long-lasting eye contact is not "allowed" in the Western European countries, but if one doesn't use this at all while face-to-face communicating with somebody, it may seem, that the speaker has something to hide or that he/she is way too shy. In contrast to this stands the Asian culture, especially the Japanese and the Chinese, where eye-contact is considered to be an indicator of an intimate relationship with the counterpart.

In this respect it should be mentioned that no doubt the ***mutually shared emotional background knowledge***, the previous emotional experience of the interlocutors, intermingles with the cognitive elements of the mind and finds an implicit way of expression in speech. Thus, the positive or negative predisposition of the interlocutors which comes from their social relationships and past emotional experience (mother – child, grandmother – granddaughter, uncle – niece, teacher – student, employer – employee, close friends, couples, spouses, etc.) enables at least one of the interlocutors (or both of them) to interpret the intended meaning positively or negatively without tracing any explicit verbal elements expressing emotive charge. In this case the emotional attitude is worked out through implicature and logical work on part the speaker and the interpreter.

Ruled by certain positive or negative emotions, speakers use both verbal means of expressing emotions, i.e. language units (words, phrases, structures, speech acts) and non-verbal means of expressing emotions, i.e. facial expressions displaying diverse emotions, gross bodily movements, different gestures, etc. carrying positive or negative implications and, in doing so, they get involved in contradictory types of interaction. In this respect, as we have said, the relationship of the speakers is of utmost importance as well. Besides, it should be mentioned that face-to-face communication greatly differs from on-line communication or phone communication, since talking without seeing each other may cause actual misunderstanding or the feel of need to express something in a more intensive and expressive way. In case of face-to-face communication, actually, both sides may express their thoughts and feelings in a very explicit manner simultaneously influencing one another. In case they display negative emotions, they consequently get involved in conflict talk, quarrel, argumentation, row, etc. In case they reveal the presence of positive emotions, their interlocutors come to think that there is a positive predisposition between them and, thus, no actual conflict communication results (Ternès, Rostomyan, 2011a,b, 2012).

Obviously, the positive/negative emotional attitude of the speaker towards the parameters of the linguistic situation is related to his/her evaluative competence, former emotional experiences and emotional background memory, as well as his/her perceptions of similar situations, which bring to self-fulfilling prophecy, and therefore, have a vital cognitive significance. Thus, we assume that the analysis of the linguistic mechanisms of verbalization of emotions, which has become quite urgent today, should be carried out on the basis of cognitive evaluation of emotivity (Paronyan, Rostomyan, 2011a,b; Rostomyan, 2013b).

Despite some unsettled theoretical issues, a consensus view is that in diverse studies of human emotions and their actual verbal and non-verbal means of communication, it is often useful and essential to know what exact facial expressions correspond to which specific emotion and to know the basic cultural differences so that not to leave some ground for misinterpretations or further misunderstandings. Besides, it is notable that many of those non-verbal means are polysemantic. For instance, as we have mentioned, eye contact which is a non-verbal means of communication can entail a great number of various implicit meanings depending on the situational context (Rostomyan 2009, 2013b).

In the next stretch of discourse which again represents a passage from crime fiction, we can observe a case of encoding negative emotions via non-verbal means of communication, namely eye contact which is detected in court. As we know, in everyday life, as a matter of fact, sometimes even merely just a gaze may be sufficient to decode the intended positive or negative emotion. In the present case, by means of eye contact the speaker performs an indirect act of reproach:

> *Scott started to walk away, but stopped when Harry said, 'Scott.' Scott turned back to the divorce lawyer. 'I'll take his money, Scott, but I'd never take your girl.'*
> **The two lawyers locked eyes**, *and Scott recalled that some years back, Harry Hankin had lost his own children in a bitter divorce.*
> *'Thanks, Harry.' (Gimenez 2007: 459)*

In the aforementioned passage Scott is going to get divorced from his wife. The speakers have been good friends for quite a long period of time and have experienced rather positive emotions towards one another. Yet Harry, who is a lawyer, has accepted to undertake the divorce case of his friend's wife for money. When Scott learns about this, he most probably feels depressed because he regards this act as treachery. So, his feelings towards his close friend change for the worse and Scott, undoubtedly, begins to experience rather negative emotions, such as disappointment, annoyance, anger. Thus, Scott turns his back on Harry to walk away, who stops him by saying that he would take the money but never his children. As a means of non-verbal communication, he was continually gazing at Scott, the two lawyers locked eyes, which is generally considered to be a sign of confidence and reliability. Of course, as far as eye contact is concerned the problem should be viewed from an intercultural or multicultural perspective. For instance, an eye contact may be a bearer of different meanings in diverse cultures; e.g. a long-lasting eye contact is not "allowed" in the Western European cultures, but if one does not use it at all while face-to-face communication, it may seem, that the speaker has something to hide or that he/she is way too shy. In contrast to this stands the Asian culture, especially the Japanese and the Chinese, where eye contact is considered to be an indicator of an intimate relationship with the counterpart. In the extract mentioned above we can regard the long-lasting eye contact as an indicator of reliability and trustfulness. Actually, this very non-verbal means of communicating emotions makes Scott recall good memories from some years back when they used to be close friends and when Harry lost his own children in a bitter divorce case. Thus, Scott, notwithstanding the actual depressing state of affairs, due to his former positive emotional background knowledge positively evaluates Harry's determination of trying to save the children for his former best friend and, as a result, he performs an expressive act of thanking. As observed in the illustrated example, the positive and negative emotional background memories always intermingle and guide in the process of interpersonal communication (Rostomyan, 2012: 289-290).

The next passage represents an extract taken from M. Gimenez's book *"The Colour of Law"* where one of the main characters, Shawanda Jones, was to be convicted for a crime she had not committed. Thus, when her lawyer, Mr. Scott Fenney, actually managed to justify her guiltless, she and many other people present in court, who believed in her innocence, displayed their genuine positive emotions through lots of non-verbal means of communicating emotions, whereas the members of the opposing side just vice versa manifested non-verbal means of communicating negative emotions.

> *Shawanda **sagged** and would have fallen to the floor if Scott had not caught her. She **buried her face in his chest and embraced him.** He held her tightly, his **tears mixing** with hers. Boo and Pajamae ran to them as the courtroom **erupted in cheers** and **shouts** and **applause.** The jurors **hugged** each other, reporters crowded Scott and Shawanda, Ray Burns sat at the prosecution table **shaking his head**, and Bobby and Karen **kissed like newlyweds.** Senator McCall pushed his way through the crowd out of the courtroom. Dan Ford sat shaking his head in wonderment at the turn of events. Shawanda **whispered** in Scott's ear, 'That a righteous name, Atticus.'*

> *Scott turned to the bench and his **eyes met** Judge Buford's. The judge **nodded** at Scott and Scott **nodded back.** (Gimenez2007: 456-457)*

In the given passage Shawanda is so impressed and astonished by the fact that she has been proven guiltless that she embraces her lawyer, Scott, and as the author describes, she might even have fallen because of anxiety. Both of them cry because of experiencing extremely strong emotions; here the tears are indicators of happiness and not sadness. Boo, Scott's child, and Pajamae, Shawanda's child, as well as everybody else positively disposed towards the accused display cheers and shouts of happiness. Even the jurors hug each other; thus, by this means of conveying positive emotions, expressing their happiness, gladness, joy, delight, cheerfulness, and other related positive emotions, whereas the representatives of the opposing side shake their heads imparting negative emotions and expressing their discontent. Shawanda performs an indirect speech act of thanking, saying Scott that Atticus is a righteous name. Actually, she is an Afro-American woman who lives in very bad conditions and is really very grateful to Mr. Scott Fenney who, in spite of being a corporate lawyer, decided to defend her without any money similar to Atticus Finch, the hero of Harper Lee's novel "To Kill a Mockingbird"; thus, following his own convictions. The Judge who appointed Scott to be Shawanda's lawyer is also satisfied with and proud of his work, and when their eyes meet, he nods at Scott; hence, by means of this non-verbal means of communication he actually performs an act of approval. Scott nods back and they understand each other without uttering any words. The decoding process of the conveyed information is carried out based on their former emotional background knowledge. As a matter of fact, referring to the linguistic and situational context we know that when at first Scott was appointed by the Judge to take the position of defending the accused, he had refused to take up the job as he was afraid to lose his job, since the accused was a person suspected in having murdered the son of his boss's closest friend who was a renowned persona of might. Nodding back to the Judge, Scott manifested his mutual positive emotions showing that he is content for having saved the accused who had not committed that crime. In this case, the coding and decoding process of their positive emotions is again performed on the basis of mutually shared emotional background knowledge (Rostomyan, 2012: 291-292).

It is also important to note that background knowledge is tightly connected with such a broad and multifaceted notion as implicature, in other words it is associated with the hidden meaning, the speaker meaning, which cannot be decoded just from the first sight. It is due to background assumptions that the speaker meaning can be understood much easier in some circumstances (Grice, 1969, 1975).

Here, Pragmatics comes to the fore, which enables us to penetrate between the lines, to try to reveal that very meaning which is not expressed so explicitly. In this connection, it should by all means be noted that context is very important in the decoding process. Another important factor that we should like to highlight and precede our discussion in that line of thought is that the relations between the speakers, their beliefs, mutual emotions, and the like are of utmost importance as well. It is due to our background emotions on a very close and beloved person that we do not get offended very much, in case that very person reprimands, reproaches us, or says something which is not that pleasant for us to hear to. Our positive background emotions connected with a particular person accompany our thought in the course of decoding and lead us in the interpretation process. And just vice versa, in case we have negative background emotions connected with this or that person, it will, actually, have an impact on our interpretation of that person's statements; we will most probably interpret the coded information negatively rather than positively, even if there is no implied negative meaning. For instance, you have succeeded in a public speaking competition and a person with whom you are in tense negative relations and you have certain negative emotional background knowledge based on some earlier events, and you know for sure that that very person envies you, and just all of a sudden, in the hour of your success he/she may approach you and say a phrase like: "*You are the best orator I have ever known,*" you will interpret it negatively, since your negative background emotions will hint you that this statement lacks the felicity condition of sincerity, even if at that moment the person does not want to attach negative implication to the statement. Or, if we take the instance of reproaching somebody, there is always the dilemma of mothers and mothers-in-law. If somebody's mother criticizes her, she will not take it too close to her heart and will not actually get offended, but in case the same disapproval of something is made on the part of the mother-in-law, the daughter-in-law will almost always get offended and seek for a thousand implied negative implications (Paronyan, Rostomyan, 2011b: 11; Rostomyan 2013b).

In summary, it should be noted that the analysis of the linguistic mechanisms of manifestation of emotions, which has become quite urgent today, should be realized on the basis of cognitive evaluation of emotivity. The positive and negative predisposition between the interlocutors plays a vital role in the process of decoding any piece of information. It should become your duty to strive towards managing the display of your emotions as an indispensable part of your profession, notwithstanding ever their negative emotional disposition, which will consequently help to create a healthier working atmosphere and ensure better results.

2.7. The Nature of Emotion Expression Management Techniques in Speech

When discussing the complexity of human emotions Andersen and Guerrero speak about five expression management techniques of emotions: 1) *intensification*, 2) *de-intensification*, 3) *simulation*, 4) *inhibition*, and 5) *masking*, with the help of which people try to handle the expression of their emotions (Andersen and Guerrero, 1998: 49-96).

The nature of the aforementioned five *expression management techniques of emotions* has been fully discussed and analyzed by extracts from English fiction by Anna Rostomyan (2013a: 141-153) published by Inter-disciplinary Press, and which are briefly presented below:

Intensification (or *maximization*) refers to creating the appearance that emotions are felt more strongly than they are. It is important to note that intensification involves the display of an emotion that is

genuinely felt; its display is simply exaggerated (see Andersen and Guerrero, 1998).

In fact, people sometimes when feeling an emotion express it more
strongly than they actually feel it. For instance, if a person is slightly
surprised, he/she may act as if the surprise is exceedingly high. Likewise, if someone feels somewhat sad, he/she may express an over-
whelming portion of grief. Other examples of intensification include
laughing generously at something which is only slightly amusing, etc. It
is also noteworthy that intensification seems to be used both with positive and negative emotions. Via intensification the speaker may basically have an emotive influence on the interlocutors, subtly suggesting
to them what emotions they should feel (Rostomyan, 2013b).

To elucidate this, let us examine the following pair of examples:
the first one represents a case of intensification bearing positive implication, whereas the second one carries overall negative implication:
1. She sat down rather stiffly in the straight-backed armchair
beside the fire.
'How pretty the fire is,' she said.
'Jeanne, I think I'm **crazily** in love with you,' said ***Andrews in
an excited voice***.
(Dos Passos, Three Soldiers, 1921: 360)

2. 'A big society party.'
'Which raises money for charity.'
'Which you ***don't give a damn*** about. It's just another step
up the Highland Park social ladder for you. You're social
climbing and Boo's being raised by Consuela!'
(Gimenez, The Colour of Law, 2007: 67)

In the first example Andrews is experiencing rather positive
emotions towards his interlocutor. As we know, there are a number of
intensifying adverbs which amplify the positive meaning of the word
they are attached to, i.e. *completely, greatly, entirely, fully, totally, extremely, tremendously, crazily, terrifically, really, truly,* etc. As a matter
of fact, intensification of speech is a permanent and highly important

feature of colloquial style. There are different ways and means of giving emotive force to a whole sentence or any part of it. Apart from the emphasis given by information theme and rheme, language provides a great number of other means of giving a sentence or a clause, or any unit of the sentence purely emotive emphasis. Here belong: stress, various kinds of intensifiers, exclamations, the emphatic *do* in declarative and imperative sentences, reduplication, emphatic syntactic structures, interjections, vocatives, expletive words, etc. (Buzarov, 1969: 66). In this case, the speaker uses the intensifying adverb *crazily* to reinforce the actual positive implication of his expressive speech act and to stress his inner positive emotional state of being in love. His positive emotions are not only manifested on the verbal level, but also on the vocal level: *said Andrews in an excited voice* (Rostomyan, 2013a: 144).

In the second example, we observe a case of negative emotional intensification. In familiar conversation between equals a few somewhat vulgar intensifiers often occur as premodifiers of adjectives or adverbs, such as *darn(ed), damn(ed), goddamn(ed), goldarn(ed)/goldurn(ed)* (a euphemistic substitution for goddamn), *bloody, hellish, all-fired(ly)* (meaning extremely) and a few others, which can also be used for both positive and negative evaluations. In the adduced extract, the intensifying adjective *damn* attaches negative emotive emphasis to the act of reproach: the conversation occurs between spouses; the husband is dissatisfied with his wife's addiction to being a renowned person in the social circles of Highland Park; hence, we may guess that he undergoes emotions belonging to the negative scale, such as resentment, anger, annoyance and the like, which are being expressed in his speech act when he reproaches his wife for not taking care of their child, Boo, and leaving the maintenance of the child only to their housemaid (Rostomyan, 2013a: 144).

In this connection, it is of paramount importance to denote that in the process of decoding any intensified utterance the felicity condition of sincerity (Searle, 1969: 66) is by all means to be taken into consideration as illustrated in the passage below:

'Mr. Fenney,' Rob said, 'your speech at the bar luncheon, it was ***truly*** inspiring.'
First day on the job and the boy was already brown-nosing like an experienced associate. Could he possibly be sincere?
'Thanks, Bob.'
Missy ***winked***. Scott didn't know if the wink was because she knew his speech was bullshit or if she was flirting again.
(Gimenez, The Colour of Law, 2007: 14)

In the aforementioned example, Mr. Scott Fenney, who has just performed an important speech at the bar luncheon, does not actually know how to decode the intensified expressive speech act uttered by Rob, who seems to be amazed by Fenney's speech. Rob attaches extra positive emotive emphasis to his expressive speech act by applying the intensifying adverb truly which preceding the adjective inspiring gives positive emotive emphasis to it; thus, intensifying the overall positive meaning of the speech act. However, as Rob is Fenney's subordinate, the latter does not really believe in the sincerity condition of the performed speech act. As for Missy, she converses with Scott via non-verbal means of communication, i.e. she winks at him. In this case Scott does not know either how to process the received information; according to the author's remarks, it can embody diverse implicit meanings, such as flirting or just subtly pointing out to the fact that Scott does not have to believe in Rob's words (Rostomyan, 2013b).

The phenomenon that every emotion is an experience involving a cognitive element, and not merely a state of feeling, can be proved by quoting McTaggart: '*We must hold that the cognition of that to which the emotion is directed, and the emotion towards it, are the same mental state, which has both the quality of being a cogitation of it, and the quality of being an emotion directed toward it.*' (McTaggart 1927: 146)

De-intensification (or minimization) refers to giving the impression that emotions are felt less strongly than they are. However, it should by all means be mentioned that only part of the felt emotion is hidden, while some portion of it is being displayed. As with intensification, de-intensification involves the display of an emotion which is genuinely felt; its display is merely softened. Actually, sometimes people feel an emotion and display it on the outside, without being able to suppress the expression of the felt emotion, yet they express it not as strongly as they feel it. For instance, if a person is angry with someone, he/she may simply exhibit mild irritation rather than revealing all of his/her anger. To illustrate this phenomenon, let us examine a situation, in which a man tries to hide his actual emotions by minimizing the degree of the experienced emotions:

> *'Look, **honey**, I'm **kind of** busy, so if everything's under control there, I need to get back to work.' (Gimenez, The Colour of Law, 2007: 35)*

It is truly obvious that the speaker feels irritated and embarrassed because of being disturbed and interrupted while working. This is the reason why he quite probably undergoes rather negative emotions at the moment of speech production. Nevertheless, he does not explicitly manifest those very negative emotions not to upset the interlocutor, who obviously is a close person to the speaker, as the latter, when addressing his interlocutor, uses the noun *honey* as a vocative expression, which is generally used to denote close rapport between equals. Besides, he uses the approximator *kind of* to minimize the degree of his categoricity and, thus, tries to minimize the overall negative emotive emphasis of the act of reproach (Rostomyan, 2013a: 145).

> The next extract from English fiction again illustrates another instance of de-intensification:
> *'**Kind of** funny, ain't it, Scotty?'*
> *'What?'*
> *'Back in school, we used to talk about working together. After all this time, we are.' He shrugged. '**Kind of** funny.'*
> *(Gimenez, The Colour of Law, 2007: 126)*

This extract represents a stretch of discourse between former best friends who used to study together and had dreamed of working as a team in the future. However, the reality turned out to be quite different from their expectations: Scott became a renowned corporate lawyer with a very high income, whereas Bobby did not manage to find a good job after graduating from the university. However, because of certain circumstances, Scott currently faces financial difficulties and cannot afford to hire a better lawyer to help him with a certain case he has been appointed to handle by the Judge. So, Bobby uses he approximator *kind of* to de-intensify the degree of his being content that they finally come to work together. Yet, the adjective *funny,* to which the approximator kind of is attached, points out to the fact that there is some irony in his speech act. Besides, he also uses a non-verbal means of communication, i.e. he *shrugs*, which also indicates that Bobby implicitly hints to that fact that life is a ladder during which we may either rise or fall, and on this very occasion the former best friends, who have been isolated from each other because of the former status gap between them, happen to be on the same stage again.

Simulation refers to displaying an emotion which is not genuinely felt. Such efforts seem to be misleading. Buller and Burgoon suggest that here deception is embodied in intentionally encoding a message by a sender to foster a false deduction by the receiver (Buller and Burgoon, 1998: 381-402). However, in contrary to its reputation, deception can be viewed as a behavioural competent in interpersonal relations. Knapp and Comadena suggest the notion of *'collaborative deception'*, which is recognized by all the parties involved and is being practiced to maintain a presumably shared desire for the smooth flow of interaction and co-operation (Knapp and Comadena, 1979: 270-285). One form of the so-called collaborative deception occurs *'when lies are used to mutually benefit the self-esteem of the participants'* (O'Hair and Cody 1994: 186). Collaborative deception seems especially related to the display rules that foster predictable social encounters. Simulation, in particular, seems likely to be used for this purpose, as it is the only management technique, which involves no genuine experience of emotion. The most frequently cited example of this emotion management technique is smiling when one does not experience such positive emotions as: gladness, happiness, joy, delight, and the like, but for collaborative peaceful interaction displays it (Rostomyan, 2013a: 145; 2013b).

Let us consider an illustration of simulation by adducing the following situation:

As the applause grew louder, the corporate tax lawyer whom Scott was campaigning to succeed as the next state bar president leaned in close and whispered, 'You know, Scotty, you've got an impressive line of bullshit. Now I see why half the coeds at SMU dropped their drawers for you.'

Scott squeezed the knot of his silk tie, smoothed his $ 2000 suit, and whispered back through brilliant white teeth, 'Henry, you don't get laid or elected telling the truth.' (Gimenez, The Colour of Law, 2007: 10)

As it can be concluded from the given passage, the speaker displays emotions, which are not genuinely felt: he smiles a big smile showing his brilliant white teeth, displaying falsified positive emotions, such as happiness, gladness, cheerfulness and other related positive emotions. As he himself explains to the corporate tax lawyer, whom he was campaigning, he merely plays sincerity in front of the audience to acquire their positive disposition towards him, since by telling the truth he won't be elected. Here, Scott adheres to the display rule of vocational requirements, since to simulate his emotions is a part-and-parcel of his profession as a lawyer. The next example again illustrates a case of simulation:

*Sid **smiled** at Bobby. 'Do all the work, like I do for Scott on Dibrell matters.'*

*Sid's **smile disappeared** when he turned to Scott and saw that Scott wasn't smiling.*

'Yeah, Sid, only difference is, I need Bobby. You can be replaced.'

*Sid **squirmed and forced a sheepish grin.***

(Gimenez, The Colour of Law, 2007: 123)

In this case, Sid simulates his truly felt emotions by displaying a *smile* on his face, which is generally considered to be a non-verbal means of communicating positive emotions (Rostomyan, 2013b). Yet, as we may guess from the context, in reality he does not feel such positive emotions as happiness, gladness, cheerfulness and the like. His smile disappears, when he understands that Scott does not buy his falsified positive disposition towards them. Then, he again displays a grin, which, according to the words of the author, is a *sheepish* one, as his truly felt negative emotions have actually been revealed by his interlocutors.

As we have mentioned, the phenomenon of simulating the emotions may have collaborative function and, in this case, it can be regarded as a very useful tool for handling the process of communicative interaction, as it can be revealed in the next stretch of discourse, where the shop assistant simulates positive emotions to satisfy the needs of the consumers:

> *Darcy tells her that I will need a complementary shade, as the maid of honor.*
> *'How nice. Sisters?'* **The woman smiles.** *Her big, square teeth remind me of Chiclets.*
> *'No,' I say.*
> *'But she's like my sister,' Darcy says,* **simply and sincerely**.
> *(Giffin, Something Borrowed, 2011: 143)*

In the given extract, Darcy wants to buy a definite shade of lipstick for herself and for her maid of honour. To attract their attention and to exhibit a pleasant appearance, the shop assistant displays positive emotions with a non-verbal marker: she smiles. Thus, the woman's smile is expressed for a positive purpose which in this case is a true part of her vocation (Rostomyan, 2013b).

Inhibition involves exposing the appearance of no emotion when in reality one is feeling a definite sort of emotion. Sometimes people feel an emotion, but do not express it for some reason. Prime examples of inhibition include keeping a straight face when something seems funny, hiding attraction towards someone, keeping a seemingly calm voice when feeling angry, etc. It has been proved by diverse linguists and psychologists that people learn to exhibit the expression of certain emotions in due course of time (Brannigan and Humphries, 1969: 406-408). This phenomenon is evidenced by the fact that often children's interactions are generally uninhibited as compared with adult interactions, as can be observed in the stretch of discourse elucidated below:

> *But Boo was quiet. Then, without looking at him, she said:*
> *'You secretly loved my mother, but she married A. Scott. You've never gotten over it. You've always wondered what your life would've been like if she had married you instead.'*
> *Bobby hadn't figured on that. He had **to take a deep breath**. He pushed himself up but looked down at her.*
> ***'How**?'*
> *'I saw how you looked at her when you got here. Your eyes went all over the crowd, kind of **frantic** like, until you saw her. Then you just looked at her for a long time. Like, forever.'*
> *Bobby walked directly to the beer cooler.*
> *(Gimenez, The Colour of Law, 2007: 172)*

Here, Boo speaks to Bobby, a friend of her father. Decoding the meaning of Booby's non-verbal behaviour, i.e. his frantic like look across the crowd searching for the mother of Boo, she understands that Bobby has been infatuated by her mother for already quite a long time. She does not strive towards inhibiting her emotions and thoughts. On the contrary, she freely and honestly expresses them. Bobby is astonished by the frankness of the child. Moreover, he does not know how to react. As we may guess from the context, at the moment of speech production Booby's felt emotions rather belong to the negative scale, such as irritation, nervousness, uneasiness, shame, and the like. So, he utters an elliptical sentence, i.e. *how*, wondering how a small girl could come up with such a precise conclusion. Hearing the child's response, Bobby feels that he is no longer capable to manage to inhibit the display of his emotions, since as we know people, when undergoing too strong emotions, do not manage to have a cognitive control over them which are consequently being manifested through verbal and/or non-verbal means of emotion expressions. Thus, not to give himself away he merely remains silent and walks directly to the beer cooler (Rostomyan, 2013b).

In contrast to child communication, while observing adult communication, we can very often reveal that in certain circumstances adults deliberately inhibit their genuine emotions as can be detected in the following illustration, which depicts an incident when one of the interactants has to hide his truly felt emotions:

> *The judge was **eyeing** Scott over his reading glasses; **a wry smile** crossed his face.*
> *'Didn't really want to be another Atticus Finch **after all**, huh, Mr. Fenney?'*
> *Scott knew better than to respond. The judge's smile dissolved into a look of disappointment that, for some odd reason bothered Scott. (Gimenez, The Colour of Law, 2007: 107)*

In the present stretch of discourse, we can truly observe that the Judge is truly dissatisfied with the work of Mr. Scott Fenney and, thus, he scolds him for not being really devoted to his lawyer's duties as Atticus Finch, the hero of Harper Lee's novel *To Kill a Mockingbird*, was, who preferred to be the lawyer of an Afro-American woman, which was out of question in those times, and to fight for justice rather than to follow the society's acknowledged norms and principles of the era. The author also implicitly hints to the Judge's discontent pointing out to his *wry* smile; the smile, being a universal sign of transmitting positive emotions, in this case is used for negative implications, hence the use of the adjective wry. He expresses an indirect act of reproach, at the end of which he adds the phrase *"after all"*, thus intensifying the overall negative implicit meaning. Scott feels embarrassed and bothered, but being conscious of the fact that he does not have to exhibit those very negative emotions in the presence of the Judge; he inhibits his genuinely felt emotions and simply remains silent to avoid subsequent tense relations with the Judge. In this case we again witness an instance of emotion management according to vocational requirements (Rostomyan, 2012: 287).

Masking differs drastically from the other management techniques in the way that it involves showing a particular emotion when one is feeling a completely different emotion. For instance, in certain circumstances a person may express happiness, when he/she feels anger. Likewise, someone may show hatred towards another person, when he/she truly loves that person. Masking is believed to be much more difficult to apply than any other emotion management technique *'probably because it is easier to moderate an existing emotion than to express an emotion that is very different from what one is feeling'* (Andersen and Guerrero, 1998: 56). This includes cases when people do not display worry and anxiety when one of their close friends or relatives has, for example, to undergo surgery. Instead, they display such emotions as felicity, hope, faith, and the like, to encourage the sick person. As it can be observed in the following example, Rachel has to mask her really felt emotions because of the existing obstacles:

> *We should hang up now. This is going in a bad direction.*
> *'Rach?'* **His voice is low and intimate**.
> *I feel breathless, hearing him say my name like this. The one*
> *syllable is familiar, warm. 'Yeah?'*
> *'You still there?' he whispers.*
> *I manage to say, 'Yes, I'm still here.'*
> *'What are you thinking?'*
> *'Nothing,' I lie.*
> *I have to lie. Because what I am thinking is; maybe you are*
> *my type just a little bit more than I once thought.*
> *(Giffin, Something Borrowed, 2011: 67)*

In the aforementioned piece of discourse, the interlocutors have previously been merely close friends. Dex is now engaged to Rachel's best friend Darcy. Thus, it bothers Rachel that her former best friend addresses her so warmly, tenderly and intimately; by only using the first syllable of her name, i.e. *Rach*, even pronouncing it in a low and cherished tone. As a result, she realizes that he has developed tender emotions towards her. Yet, she does not know how to respond properly since although she undergoes similar delicate positive emotions towards him, analyzing her emotions cognitively and not letting the emotional part of her brain overrule the rational one, she masks her truly felt positive emotions, giving the appearance that she is cool, chilly, serene, since she is well-aware of the fact that she is not allowed to express her attraction towards the fiancé of her best friend, Darcy. This is the very reason why she intentionally hampers the encoding process of her real emotions not to ruin their friendship (Rostomyan, 2013a: 147-148).

In the next example, we may again observe a case of masking the emotions:

> *'This won't affect your position in the firm?'*
> *Upon retiring to the master suite, that was Rebecca's first and only question, her way of asking,* ***Will this affect your income?***
> *'No, of course not. I'm still Tom Dibrell's lawyer.'*
> ***Her expression said she wasn't buying it.***
> *'Rebecca, look, I've got Bobby working the case. He'll get me through it, she'll get convicted, and things will go back to normal. Don't worry.'*
> ***But Scott was worried.*** *That feeling of impending doom had grown stronger. (Gimenez, The Colour of Law, 2007: 128)*

As we may see, the wife, Rebecca, is worried about the probable reduction of her husband's income. As a matter of fact, Scott himself is also worried about the same issue, as the author's remark indicates. In fact, the state of affairs is such that Scott has been appointed to handle a case, which may very possibly harm his career as a successful corporate lawyer. Yet, he tries to mask his emotions, striving towards displaying a seemingly unworried description of the situation not to give ground for his wife to worry more than she does. Nonetheless, it is visible that it is very hard for him to mask his real emotions as, notwithstanding his efforts to mask his emotions, the feeling of impending doom grows stronger. However, according to the author's remark, on the non-verbal level the wife shows via her facial expression that she did not believe in his words.

It is noteworthy that emotion expression management techniques are applied different according to the culture and personal preferences. In fact, these are governed by previous emotional experiences and largely also according to certain pre-learnt patterns.

We have carried out a cross-cultural research within a group of 25-45year-old 50 people trying to reveal which emotion management technique they mostly adhere to when experiencing such basic emotions as *happiness, anger*, and *sadness*.

After having presented to them the essence of each management technique, a questionnaire was distributed to them to fill in. Of course, each nation has its own characteristics and the picture will not be exactly the same while examining the peculiarities of emotion management techniques for definite cultures and sub-cultures.

For instance, it is generally believed that the Armenians, Italians and the Spanish generally do not strive towards handling or suppressing their felt strong emotions and they express them in a very vivid manner, whereas the English, the Swiss and the Germans are believed to try to manage the expression of their even very strong emotions. This is something culturally and religiously bound, as, for instance, the protestants are to handle the expression of their strongly felt emotions as their religion does not allow it.

Anyhow, the results, illustrated in *Table 1*, come to suggest that with each emotion generally one of the discussed expression management techniques of emotions tends to prevail; namely, anger is mostly being inhibited or suppressed because of social cooperative norms, the same holds true for sadness not to sadden your dear ones, while happiness is generally being intensified across cultures and situations, presumably in order to have a positive impact on your interactants.

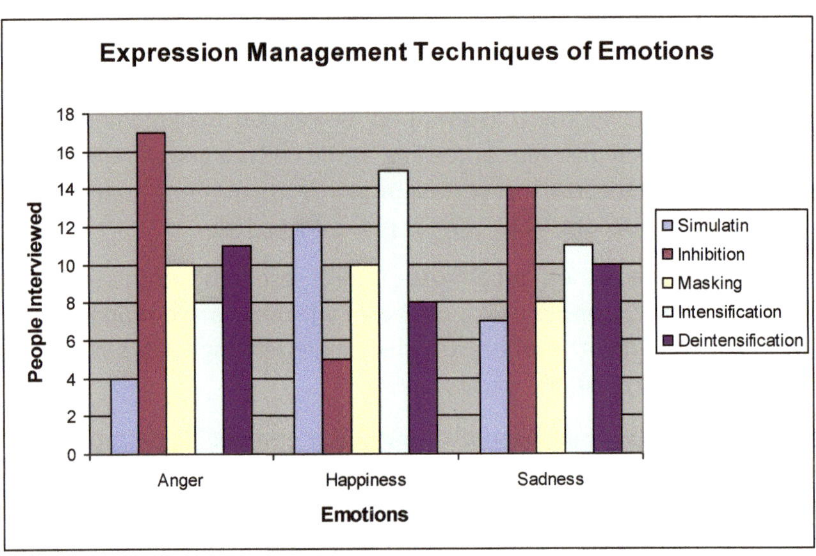

Table 1: The Ratio of the Emotion Expression Management Techniques with Anger, Happiness, and Sadness

(Table source: Rostomyan, 2013a: 148)

Indeed, people are generally believed to attempt to control the expression of their emotions: overt bodily movements, facial expressions, as well as vocal and verbal means of expressing emotivity, according to predefined display rules. The discussed display rules and expression management techniques of emotions provide universal specific tools used to avoid speech conflicts and, as an outcome, to reach an integration of the emotive and rational higher cognitive processes. Thus, by means of analyzing our emotions cognitively and handling them correspondingly, we stand a better chance of reaching communicative conflict reduction and establishing peaceful relations with the members of the given speech community.

Notwithstanding the wide capacity of the emotion expression management techniques, it is notable that before trying to handle the outward expression of this or that very emotion, one should strive towards rationalizing the nature of that inner emotion, try to analyze both the negative and positive effects of it on the surroundings. It follows that by means of using the emotions properly one can enhance his or her thinking abilities, reaching the point of both perceiving and understanding emotions, which can lead to gaining a rational control over emotions and managing their actual expression, which can consequently develop strong communication skills.

Summarizing, it should be noted that each of the organizations' policies, induction procedures, performance management programs, training and operational manuals display the company's ability to educate, support and monitor the team's performance against the manager's goals and their capability. In case the manager is able to evaluate and re-evaluate his/her personal relations with the staff members and their interpersonal emotions and manages to control the display of over-negative emotions in the heat of the emotional moment, trying to express those very emotions in a more diplomatic way, he/she will actually manage to have a more successful team and an even healthier working atmosphere.

2.8. The Importance of Anger Management at Workplace

In our everyday life we are continually interacting with each other. We do this with the help of linguistic and non-linguistic, verbal and non-verbal means such as facial expressions, gestures, gross bodily movements. Undoubtedly, to build a successful society and peaceful relations with one another, it is essential not to misinterpret any piece of information encoded by a speaker. As a matter of fact, people do not always communicate with each other in an explicit manner and it very often becomes a real challenge to grasp the implicit meaning, the hidden thoughts and intentions of the speaker which are actually not so vividly expressed in speech.

At workplace especially people very often are under the influence of intense negative emotions because of stressful situations and events. There is an urgency to suppress those very emotions not to harm the harmonious relations with the colleagues, relatives and friends. This is an issue that requires much effort and should be done in a way not to harm the self of the individuum as always vetoing the display of emotions can bring to sustainable harm which can be only hindered by means of healthy emotion management (Rostomyan, 2015).

By means of establishing a cognitive dominance over our strongly felt emotions we do stand a good chance to raise our Emotional Intelligence (mostly known as EQ) and to become much more proficient communicators, which will consequently ensure better behaviour development, which in its turn will greatly contribute to the development, prosperity and opulence of any business at hand.

Let us bring an extract taken from the movie "Anger Management" starring Adam Sandler and Jack Nicholson where Nicholson plays the role of a therapist who takes pains in helping his client, Sandler, to overcome his anger. The story unfolds in a way that the main character of Adam Sandler always suppressed his negative emotions, which had a great negative impact on his both personal and professional life, as he never expressed his felt emotions and became emotionally dumb.

As a result, his girlfriend grew distant and emotionally detached from him, as he was always under tension when expressing his emotions in public. Yet, after undergoing the anger management therapy, at the end of the movie the character of Adam Sandler confesses that he the doctor had helped him greatly and that he is happy to have overcome his anger displays, which helped him to harmonize his relations both at work and with his beloved woman to whom he could already express his emotions freely, which resultantly helped them grew closer in the romantic relationship. Actually, when the character of Adam learnt how to deal with his emotions, it helped him heal and respond to the outer world situations accordingly, not being ashamed of his felt very own emotions.

The thing is that in case we suppress and inhibit our emotions (both positive and negative) all the time, we will eventually have a harmed and damaged psychology. Emotions are, in fact, there for us to help us direct and manage our lives appropriately; they give us impulses how to act and react to the outward stimuli, and we have to understand and deal with them not to get into confusing situations and not to harm our very own selves.

If we compare this to films, we can state that our emotions can be understood as "Jumanji", a fantasy adventure film starring Robin Williams directed by Joe Johnston shot back in 1995 based on the 1981 children's book by Chris Van Allsburg.

In fact, if we do not tune with our emotions, deal with them, understand them and tame them appropriately, they will become a real dangerous jungle for us, which will eventually turn to an unstoppable adventurous scenario with unforeseeable negative results.

We can draw a parallel between those very situations: for example, in real life a lion can be compared to our heated emotions as anger, fury, rage, etc. Among other animals, monkeys, for instance, may represent our excitements, spiders - our irritations, because of some other outer world-based stimuli, which may cause the arousal of diverse inner states and feelings. The lion can also represent your former emotional experiences and wounds, which are ready to tear you up, in case you do not tame them in time. So, you can close it in a room, as in the movie, but it will still be there, and hence, you have to learn appropriate strategies to deal with them accordingly.

When speaking about workplace, in case both the managers and the employees manage to handle their negative emotions appropriately, and express them in a predefined manner according to the demands of their profession, their colleagues, co-workers, relatives and even family and friends will consequently notice the positive change of the mood and will comment on it by means of diverse verbal and non-verbal means of communicating emotions as can be observed in the following example:

One of the interlocutors smiles imagining how he could succeed in his work. As we know a *smile* is a non-verbal means of transmitting positive emotions. Carla comments on her interlocutors' positive state of mind expressing how well the latter would feel after having succeeded in his work, i.e. putting his arm around his client, which is a non-verbal means of expressing closeness, gladness, and other people slapping him on the back, which also indicates a non-verbal means of expressing positive predisposition and congratulation. The intensifying adverb *"exactly"*, which is here used to indicate the overall positive evaluation of the situation given by the speaker.

Before reacting to anger, one should try to rationalize the outward situation. For instance, listen before reacting, count to at least four, and diminish the expression of a disastrous emotion not to harm the subsequent relations within the social community. It follows that by means of suppressing the degree of anger one can reach peace, harmony, accord with one's own self which will consequently smoothen the outside relations with the social community. As a result, this will undoubtedly lead to competence development and considerable business success in all the fields of human activity.

We do firmly believe that for every manager it should be a part of his/her profession to control his/her body language together with his/her speech, in addition checking the verbal and non-verbal behaviour of his/her employees, especially on the emotional level. Thus, having a clear-cut idea about when, where, why and why to appropriately to manage the expression of emotions via verbal and non-verbal means of communication, as well as having clear and well-defined systems, policies and procedures, including regular feedback and performance appraisals, managers will enable the working team to meet the company's, as well as their own expectations and developments.

To conclude with, our firm belief is that it is the task of each and every successful manager to link the top to the bottom of the organizational staff members and to foster a healthy working atmosphere which will offer and ensure encouragement, motivation, promotion and productivity. For this very reason, the manager should bear in mind to be calculable for his employees and try to arrange as many meetings as possible struggling to face-to-face build a stronger relationship with trust and plain messages, giving the employees the ability to share their thoughts, ideas, needs and worries, together trying to find the best solutions. Besides, the most vital keywords for cooperation should be Peace, Unity, Trust, Respect, Love and Devotion towards whatever Business you are engaged in which will consequently ensure better results. Actually, while interacting with each other there is much more going on beneath the surface than one could imagine, and in case managers and employers pay more attention the importance and vitality of human emotions, realize that they are dealing with *human* resources and not merely working machines, which are devoid of emotions, they will stand a better chance of avoiding conflicts at workplace which will consequently ensure better labour output.

CONCLUSION

One of the main beliefs of this books is that anyone and everyone can become a successful communicator, thence building strong and lasting both business and personal relationships.

It is our firm belief that by means of mastering efficient communication strategies and applying them in real-life situation one can stand a great chance of succeeding in this life.

The book gives a general overview on communication theory and provides you with practical pieces of advice, which you can apply in handling effective communication management. Moreover, the book puts a light on emotional intelligence issues, which bring to successful emotion management, as without proper emotion management we can lose track of our relationships.

Therefore, emotion display manifestation and regulation techniques should be paid their truly deserved attention to, which are well-described in the present manuscript alongside with numerous supportive examples.

Our research has also shown that emotion management and accurate emotional labour should be on the agenda of both the employers and the employees in their interpersonal communicative interrelations.

In summary, business environment increasingly grows rapidly developing, where human capital has become the utmost important factor. Hence, fundamental communication health issues come to the forefront and the role of emotions gains its paramount prominence. Therefore, it has truly become the urgency of emotional labour on the part of both the employers and employees, especially nowadays, to pay a great attention and to give its proper significance to communicative emotion expression management techniques, which are thoroughly discussed in the present book.

In fact, decision making processes are also greatly affected by the positive and negative emotions of the speaking partners and interactants, which we all should obviously be well-aware of. Thus, in case we learn the communication management techniques and strategies described in this book, we will enhance our emotional intelligence and consequently reach better results both in our personal and professional lives.

To conclude with, we highly advise everybody to become open communicators and learn more in building successful interrelations.

BIBLIOGRAPHY:

1. Andersen, Peter and Guerrero, Laura (1998). 'Principles of Communication and Emotion in Social Interaction.' In *Handbook of Communication and Emotion*, edited by Peter A. Andersen and Laura K. Guerrero. San Diego: Academic Press, pp. 49-96.
2. Arnold, M. B. (1960). *Emotion and personality*. Volume I: *Psychological Aspects*. New York: Columbia University Press.
3. Austin, J.L. (1962). *How to Do Things with Words*. Oxford: Oxford University Press, 192 pages.
4. Backman, Carl. (1985). 'Identity, Self-presentation, and the Resolution of Moral Dilemmas: Toward a Social Psychological Theory of Moral Behaviour.' In *The Self and Social Life*, edited by B. L. Schlenker. New York: McGraw-Hill, pp. 261-289.
5. Baker, Carlos (1963). *Hemingway: The Writer as Artist*, 3rd ed. New Jersey: Princeton University Press.
6. Bolton, S. C. (2005). *Emotion Management in the Workplace*. Management, Work and Organisations, Palgrave.
7. Brannigan, Christopher and Humphries, David. (1969). 'I See What You Mean,' *New Scientist*, 42, pp. 406-408.
8. Bradberry, Travis & Greaves, Jean (2016). *Emotionale Intelligenz 2.0: erhoehen Sie Ihre Sozialkompetenz und verbessern Sie Ihre Kommunikation*. Muenchen: mvg Verlag.
9. Brown, R. (2009). *Public Relations and the Social Web: How to Use Social Media and Web 2.0 in Comunications*. London: Kogan Page.
10. Bugental, J.F.; Wegrocki, H. J.; Murphy, G.; Thomae, H.; Allport, G.W.; Ekstein, R.; Garvin, P.L. (1966). Symposium on Karl Bühler's Contributions to Psychology. *The Journal of General Psychology* 75 (2d Half): pp. 181–219.
11. Bühler, K. (1999). *Sprachtheorie. Die Darstellungsfunktion der Sprache*. Mit einem Geleitw. von Friedrich Kainz. - 3. Aufl. - Stuttgart: G. Fischer,. - XXXIV, 434 S. (UTB für Wissenschaft; 1159), hier: S. 24-33.
12. Buller, David and Burgoon, Judee (1998). 'Emotional Expression in the Deception Process.' In *Handbook of Communication*

and Emotion, edited by Peter A. Andersen and Laura K. Guerrero. San Diego, CA: Academic Press, pp. 381-402.

13. Burgoon, Judee (1993). 'Interpersonal Expectations, Expectancy Violations, and Emotional Communication,' *Journal of Language and Social Psychology*, 12, pp. 30-48.

14. Buzarov, V. V. (1998). *Essentials of Conversational English Syntax*. Moscow: Crone-press.

15. Callahan, J. L. (2000). 'Emotion management and organizational functions: A case study of patterns in a not-for-profit organization'. *Human Resource Development Quarterly*, Volume 11, 3. pp. 245-267.

16. Camras, Linda (1982). 'Socialization of Affect Communication.' In *The Socialization of Emotions*, edited by M. Lewis and C. Saari. New York: Plenum Press, pp. 141-160.

17. Carnegie, Dale (1982). *How to Win Friends and Influence People*. New York, London, Toronto, Sydney: Pocket Books.

18. Castells, M. (2007). Communication, Power and Counter-power in the Network Society. *International Journal of Communication* 1.

19. Cicero, *De Oratore*, trans. by W. B. Owen, Boston, 1895, p. 101.

20. Clore G., Ortony A. (2000). *Cognition in Emotion: Always, Sometimes, or Never?* Series in affective science. *Cognitive Neuroscience of Emotion*. R. Lane and L. Nadel (Eds.) NY: Oxford University Press, pp. 24–61.

21. Coleman, J. S. (1990). *Foundations on Social Theory*. Massachussetts: The Belknap Press and Harward University Press.

22. Damasio, A. (1994). *Descartes' Error: Emotion, Reason, and the Human Brain*. New York: G.P. Putnam's Sons.

23. Damasio, A. (1999). *The Feeling of what Happens: Body and Emotion in the Making of Consciousness*. New York: Harcourt Brace and Co.

24. Dennett, D. (1989). *The Neurobiology of Memory: Concepts, Findings, Trends*. New York: Oxford University Press.

25. Dennett, D. *Consciousness Explained*. New York: Little Brown, 1991.

26. De Sousa, R. (1987). *The Rationality of Emotion*. Cambridge MA: MIT Press.

27. Deutsch, M. (1958). "The Effects of Motivational Orientation upon Trust and Suspicion", *Human Relations*, vol. 13 Sage Publications, pp. 123-139.
28. Dijk, Teun A. van, and Kintsch W. (1977a). *Cognitive Psychology and Discourse*. In: W.U. Dressier, ed. Current trends in text linguistics. Berlin, New York: de Gruyter.
29. Dijk, Teun A. van. (1977b). *Text and Context. Explorations in the semantics and pragmatics of discourse*. London: Longmans.
30. Dos Passos, John (1921). *Three Soldiers*. New York: Modern Library.
31. Ekman, Paul (1979). *About Brows: Emotional and Conversational Signals*. In M. von Cranach, K. Foppa, W. Lepenies, D. Ploog (Eds), *Human Ethology*: Claims and Limits of a New Discipline: Contributions to the Colloquium, Cambridge: Cambridge University Press, pp. 169-248.
32. Ekman, Paul (2004). *Emotions Revealed: Recognizing Faces and Feelings to Improve Communication*. New York: Henry Holt and Company.
33. Ekman, Paul and Friesen, Wallace (1975). *Unmasking the Face: A Guide to Recognizing Emotions from Facial Clues*. Englewood Cliffs, NJ: Prentice-Hall.
34. Ekman, Paul, Friesen, Wallace and Ellsworth, Phoebe (1972). *Emotion in the Human Face: Guidelines for Research and an Integration of Findings*. New York: Pergamon Press.
35. Fineman, St. (Ed.) (2008). *The Emotional Organization: Passions and Power*. Blackwell: Malden.
36. Fineman, St. (Ed.) (2000). *Emotion in Organizations*. Sage: London.
37. Friedemann, S. von Thun (1981). *Miteinander reden 1 – Störungen und Klärungen. Allgemeine Psychologie der Kommunikation*. Rowohlt: Reinbek.
38. Friedemann, S. von Thun (Hrsg.), Johannes Ruppel, Roswitha Stratmann (2000). *Miteinander reden: Kommunikation für Führungskräfte*. Rowohlt: Reinbek.
39. Giffin, E. (2011). *Something Borrowed*. London: Arrow Books.
40. Gimenez, M. (2007). *The Colour of Law*. London: Sphere.

41. Goldie, P. (2000). *The Emotions: A Philosophical Exploration.* New York, Oxford: Oxford University Press.

42. Goleman, D. (1995). *Emotional Intelligence.* New York, Toronto, London, Sydney, Auckland: Bantam Books.

43. Graves, R.H. (1934). *The Triumph of an Idea: The Story of Henry Ford.* New York: Country Life Press.

44. Grice, H.P. (1969). *Utterer's Meaning and Intentions.* Philosophical Review, New York: Academic Press.

45. Grice, H.P. (1975). *Logic and Conversation.* In P. Cole & J. Morgan (Eds). Syntax and semantics, Vol. 3, New York: Academic Press.

46. Griffiths, P.E. (1997). *What Emotions Really Are.* London, Chicago: Chicago University Press.

47. Grisham, John (2005). *A Time to Kill.* New York: Bantam Dell.

48. Hartley, P. (1993). *Interpersonal Communication.* London: Routledge.

49. Heritage, J. (2005). *Cognition in Discourse.* Conversation and Cognition. H.te Moulder et al. Eds., Cambridge: Cambridge University Press.

50. Hochschild, A. R. (1983). *The Managed Heart: Commercialization of human feeling.* Berkeley: University of California Press.

51. Hochschild, A. R. (1990). *Research Agendas in the Sociology of Emotions.* SUNY series in the sociology of emotions. Albany, NY, US: State University of New York. pp. 117-142.

52. Hsieh, T. (2010). *Delivering Happiness: A Path to Profits, Passion, and Purpose.* New York, Boston: Business Plus Press.

53. Hutton, Chris (2009). *Language, Meaning and the Law.* Edinburgh: Edinburgh University Press.

54. James, W. (1890). *The Principles of Psychology.* Classics in the History of Psychology. An internet resource developed by Christopher D. Green of York University. Toronto, Ontario.

55. Kasevich, B.V. (1989). *Yazikovie structuri i kognitivnaya deyatel'nost'.* P.M.Frumkinoy (Ed.). Moskva, in-m yazikoznaniya AN SSSR.

56. Knapp, Mark and Comadena, Mark (1979). 'Telling It Like It Isn't: A Review of Theory and Research on Deceptive Communications,' *Human Communication Research*, 5, pp. 270-285.

57. Kohring, M., & Matthes, J. (2007). 'Trust in news media: Development and validation of a multidimensional scale'. *Communication Research*, 34(2), 231-252.

58. Leyens, J., Rodriguez-Perez, A. et alia (2001). European Journal of Social Psychology, Wiley On Line Library, 31(4), pp. 395–411.

59. Levinson, S.C., (1983). *Pragmalinguistics*. Cambridge, UK: Cambridge University Press.

60. Lively, K. J. (2000). 'Reciprocal Emotion Management: Working Together to Maintain Stratification in Private Law Firms'. *Work and Occupations*, 27. pp. 32 – 63.

61. Malatesta, Carol and Izard, Carroll (1984). 'Conceptualizing Emotional Development in Adults.' In *Emotion in Adult Development*, edited by Carol Zander Malatesta and Carroll Ellis Izard. Beverly Hills: Sage Publications, pp. 13-21.

62. Malinowski, B. (1923). The Problem of Meaning in Primitive Languages. In *The Meaning of Meaning: A Study of Influence of Language Upon Thought and of the Science of Symbolism*. C. K. Ogden and I. A. Richards. New York: Harcourt, Brace and World, pp. 296-336.

63. Matsumoto, David (1991). 'Cultural Influences on Facial Expressions on Emotion,' *Southern Communication Journal: Patterns and Functions of Nonverbal Communication*, 56, pp. 128-137.

64. McTaggart, John Ellis (1927). *The Nature of Existence*. Vol. 2. Cambridge: Cambridge University Press.

65. Murray, E.J. (1964). *Motivation and Emotion*. New Jersey: Prentice-Hall, Inc.

66. Murray, I.R., Arnott J.L. (1993). *Toward the simulation of emotion in synthetic speech: a review of the literature of human vocal emotion*. In J. Acoust. Soc. Am., vol. 93(2), pp. 1097-1108.

67. Neale, M.A., Bazerman, M.H. (1994) *Negotiating* Rationality. *Journal of Business and Economics*, NY: Simon and Schuster, 196 p.

68. Nussbaum, M. (2001). *Upheavals of Thought: The Intelligence of Emotions*. Cambridge: Cambridge University Press, 766 p.
69. Ochsner, K.N., Gross, J. J. (2005). The Cognitive Control of Emotion. *Trends in Cognitive Sciences*, Vol.9, No.5. Amsterdam: Elsevier Ltd, pp. 242-249.
70. O'Hair, Dan and Cody, Michael (1994). 'Deception.' In *The Dark Side of Interpersonal Communication*, edited by William R. Cupach and Brian H. Spitzberg. Hillsdale, NJ: Lawrence Erlbaum, pp. 181-213.
71. Oxford Advanced Learner's Dictionary (1997). Oxford: Oxford University Press.
72. Paronyan, Sh. (2011). *Lezvachanachoghutyun ev diskurs*, Yereven: YSU Press.
73. Paronyan, Sh., Rostomyan, A. (2011a). On the Interrelation between Cognitive and Emotional Minds in Speech. Armenian Folia Anglistika, *International Journal of English Studies*, 1-2(8), Yerevan: Lusakn Publishers, pp 26-33.
74. Paronyan, Sh., Rostomyan, A. (2011b). The Pragmatic Impact of Background Emotional Memory on Interpersonal Relations. Armenian Folia Anglistika, *International Journal of English Studies*, 2(9), Yerevan: Lezvakan Horizon, pp. 7-14.
75. Putman R. D. (2000). *Bowling Alone: The Collapse and Revival of American Community*. New York: Harper Collins.
76. Quandt, Throsten (2012). 'What's lest of trust in a network society? An evolutionary model and critical discussion of trust and societal communication'. In: Peter Golding, Helena Sousa, Liesbet van Zoonen (Eds.) *European Journal of Communication*, volume 27 (1), UK: Sage Publications Ltd., pp. 7-21.
77. Rick, S. and Loewenstein, G. (2008). *Handbook of Emotions*, Third Edition, edited by Michael Lewis, Jeannette M. Haviland-Jones, and Lisa Feldman Barrett. US: The Guilford Press, pp. 138–156.
78. Rostomyan, Anna (2009). *Means of Expressing Emotive Emphasis in Conversational English*. Foreign Languages in Armenia, N10, Yerevan: YSU Press.

79. Rostomyan, Anna (2010). Emotions in Linguistic Behaviour. Armenian Folia Anglistika. *International Journal of English Studies*, 1-2(7). Yerevan: Lusakn Publishers, pp. 102-109.

80. Rostomyan, Anna (2012). *The Vitality of Emotional Background Knowledge in Court*, Polemos, 6(2), De Grutyer, pp. 281-292.

81. Rostomyan, Anna (2013a) Management Techniques of Emotions in Communicative Conflict Reduction, in part 3: Communication and Management, *Communication: Breakdowns and Breakthroughs*, Probing the Boundaries, eds. Anabel Ternès, Inter-disciplinary Press, UK: Oxford, pp.141-151.

82. Rostomyan, Anna (2013b). *Huyzeri khoskayin ev voch khoskayin drsevorumnere vorpes lezvachanachoghakan qnnutyan ararka (angleren nyuti himan vra)*/ A Linguo-cognitive Analysis on the Verbal and Non-verbal Expressions of Emotions (on the material of English fiction and films), dissertation, 160 pages, summary 27 pages, Yerevan, Armenia.

83. Rostomyan, Anna (2014). *"The Impact of Emotions in Marketing Strategy"*, in the series of scientific papers "International Trends in Brand Communication: fostering globalization, new media and sustainability"/"Internationale Trends in Markenkommunikation", Eds. Anabel Ternès and Ian Towers, Berlin: Springer Gabler, pp. 119-131.

84. Rostomyan, A. and Sukiasyan, M. (2015). *"The Importance of Emotional Intelligence in*

Neuroleadership", Finance & Economics Journal, proceedings of the conference, Frankfurt am Main, Germany.

85. Rostomyan, Anna (2015). *"The Impact of Emotions in Decision making Processes in the Field of Neuroeconomics"*, Volume 6, Number 7, Academic Star Publishing Company, New York, USA, pp. 1268-1277.

86. Rostomyan, Anna, and Rostomyan, Armen (2018). Emotional Intelligence and Leadership,

Journal of Managerial Studies and Research, 6(8), pp. 34-41.

87. Sanders, R.E. (2005). Validating "Observations" *in Discourse studies: a Methodological Reason for Attention to Cognition.*

Conversation and Cognition. H. te Moulder et al. Eds., Cambridge: Cambridge University Press.

88. Schulz von Thun, F. (1981). *Miteinander reden.Bd. 1. Störungen und Klärungen. Allgemeine Psychologie der Kommunikation*. Reinbek: Rowohlt.

89. Schulz von Thun, F. (2011). *Miteinander redden. Bd. 2. Werte und Persönlichkeitsentwicklung. Differenzielle Psychologie der Kommunikation*. Sonderausgabe. Reinbek: Rowohlt.

90. Schulz von Thun, F. (1998). *Miteinander reden. Bd. 3. Das "Innere Team" und situationsgerechte Kommunikation*. Reinbek: Rowohlt.

91. Schulz von Thun, F., Ruppel, J. & Stratmann, R. (Hrsg.) (2003). *Miteinander reden: Kommunikation für Führungskräfte*. Reinbek: Rowohlt.

92. Schulz von Thun, F. (2004). *Klarkommen mit sich selbst und anderen: Kommunikation und soziale Kompetenz: Reden, Aufsätze, Dialoge*. Reinbek: Rowohlt.

93. Searle, J.R. (1969). *Speech Acts: An Essay in The Philosophy of Language*. Cambridge, UK: Cambridge University Press.

94. Searle, J.R. (1975). *Indirect Speech Acts*. In P. Cole & J. Morgan (Eds). Syntax and Semantics, Vol. 3, New York: Academic Press.

95. Sloan, M. M. (2012). 'Unfair Treatment in the Workplace and Worker Well-Being: The Role of Coworker Support in a Service Work Environment'. *Work and Occupation*, 39, pp. 3-34.

96. Solomon, R. C. (1980). *Emotions and Choice. Explaining Emotions*, Amélie Rorty (Ed.). Los Angeles: University of California Press.

97. Solomon, R. C. (1999). *A Passion for Wisdom: A Very Brief History of Philosophy*. Oxford: Oxford University Press.

98. Solomon, R. C. (1993). *The Passions: Emotions and the Meaning of Life*. Indianapolis, IN: Hackett Pub Co.

99. Ternès, A., and Rostomyan, A., (2011a). *"Echtheit, Wahrheit, Ehrlichkeit: Die ethische Frage nach ‚Authentizität' in der computervermittelten Kommunikation*. Hochschule für Philosophie

München. Jahrestagung der DGPuK-Fachgruppen Kommunikations- und Medienethik und Computervermittelte Kommunikation und des Netzwerks Medienethik.

100.　　Ternès, A. & Rostomyan, A., (2011b). *Emotion Management in Business Ethics*. Living Responsibly Reflecting on the Ethical Issues of Everyday Life. Proceedings of the 2nd global conference on Managerial Studies organized by Inter-disciplianry.net. Prague.

101.　　Ternès, A. & Rostomyan, A., (2012). *Gefeuert wegen Facebook: Mitarbeiterkommunikation im Internet als Form von Unternehmenskommunikation.* Draft paper for the Workshop der Kommission Wissenschaftstheorie und Ethik in der Wirtschaftswissenschaft in Kooperation mit der Kommission Hochschulmanagement, Februar 2012, Freie Universität Berlin.

102.　　Ternès, A., and Rostomyan, A. (2014). *Communication and Ethics in Germany and Armenia: What ethical responsibilities do teachers have in education management?* Vol. 2 No. 3, International Journal of Education and Research, Australia, pp. 145-174.

103.　　Ternès, Anabel, Rostomyan, Anna, Gursch, Francesca, and Gursch, Giulia (2014). *"Levers of Personal Branding to Optimize Success"*, Volume 5, Number 1, Academic Star Publishing Company, USA, New York, pp. 86-94.

104.　　Verschueren, Jef (1999). *Understanding Pragmatics.* Amsterdam: Hodder Education Publishers.

105.　　Watzlawick, P., Beavin, J.H., Jackson, D. D. (1969). *Menschliche Kommunikation – Formen, Störungen, Paradoxien.* Bern: Huber.

106.　　Williams, M. (2007). Building Genuine Trust through Interpersonal Emotion Management: A Threat Regulation Model of Trust and Collaboration across Boundaries. *The Academy of Management Review Archive.* Vol. 2, No. 2. pp. 595 – 621.

107.　　Yule, G. (1996). *Pragmalinguistics*, Oxford Introductions to Language Study, series editor H. G. Widdowson. Oxford, New York: Oxford University Press.